THAT'S
FACTS-INATING!

HUMAN BODY

Kidsbooks®

Kidsbooks®

Copyright © 2016, 2019 Kidsbooks, LLC
3535 West Peterson Avenue
Chicago, IL 60659

Every effort has been made to ensure all information in this book is correct.

Printed in China
101901032GD

Visit us at www.kidsbookspublishing.com

DO YOU KNOW...

WOMEN breathe faster than **men?**

Exercise can make you **smarter?**

Human **bones** are **stronger** than **steel?**

Get ready to learn **tons** of other **fascinating facts** in this **fun-filled book** about **the human body!**

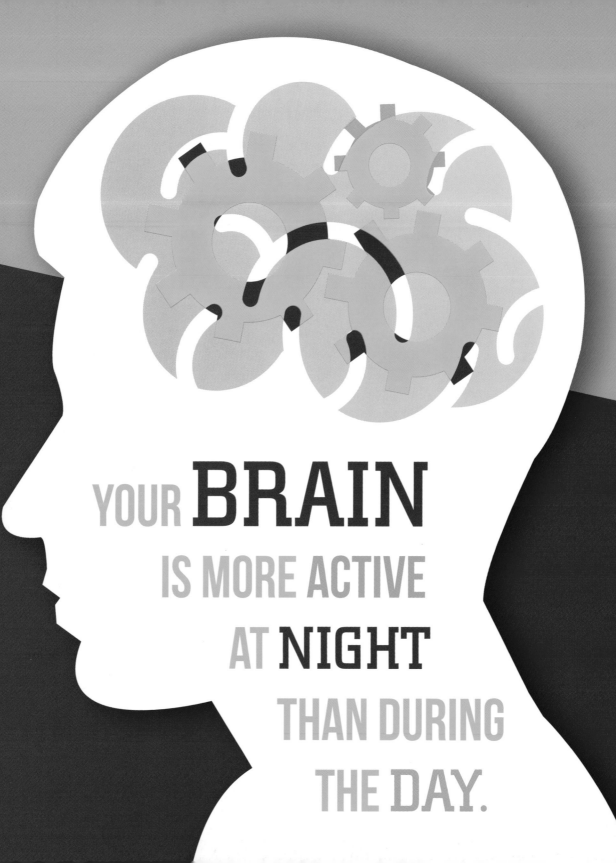

YOUR **BRAIN** IS MORE ACTIVE AT **NIGHT** THAN DURING THE DAY.

Your **TONGUE** is one of the **STRONGEST** muscles in your body.

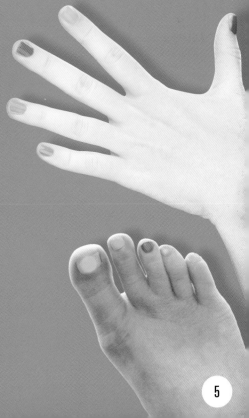

FINGERNAILS GROW FASTER THAN TOENAILS.

ADULTS have fewer BONES than

BABIES because, as babies grow, their BONES grow together.

Your ♥ beats *about* **100,000** times a day.

GRAVITY MAKES YOUR **NOSE** AND **EARS** DROOP OVER TIME, SO THEY APPEAR TO NEVER STOP **GROWING.**

Most dreams are forgotten **minutes** after **waking.**

It is almost impossible to SNEEZE with your eyes open.

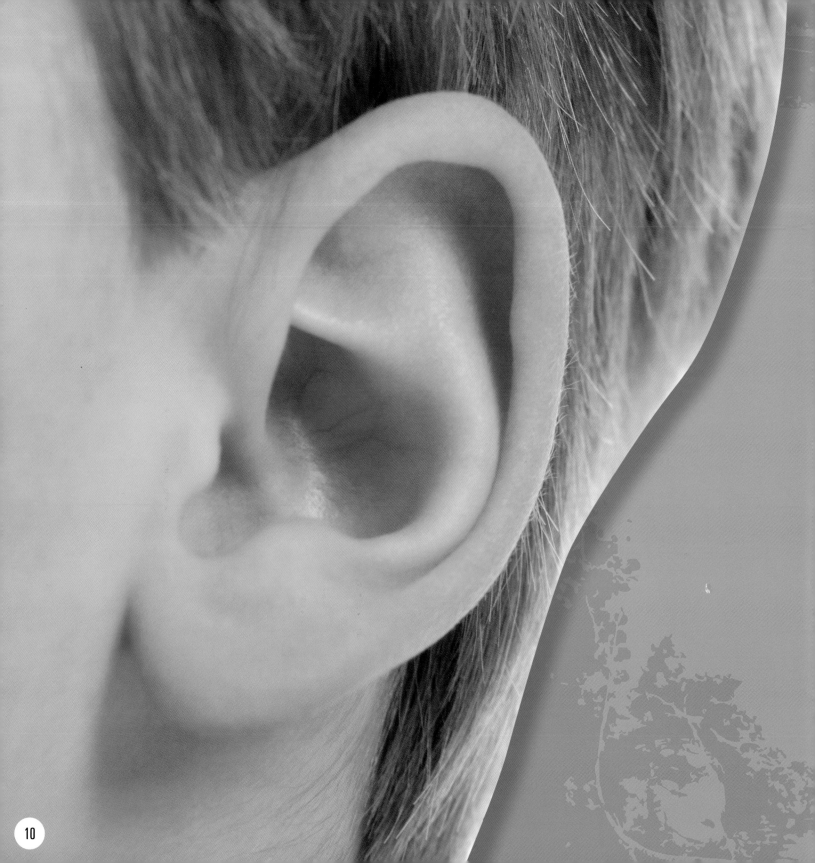

The **WAX** in your ears prevents **DUST** and even small bugs from getting inside.

Eeeew!

Natural blondes have more hair than brunettes. Redheads have the least amount of hair.

People have about the same amount of hairs on their bodies as

CHIMPANZEES.

The hairs on humans are just finer and harder to see.

13

It takes more effort to

FROWN

than it does to

SMILE.

YOUR BODY IS MADE UP MOSTLY OF WATER.

Chickens don't cause **CHICKEN POX**; a **VIRUS** causes chicken pox.

ON AVERAGE, **BEARDS** GROW **5.5 INCHES** PER **YEAR.**

The hardest **BONE** in your body is your **jawbone.**

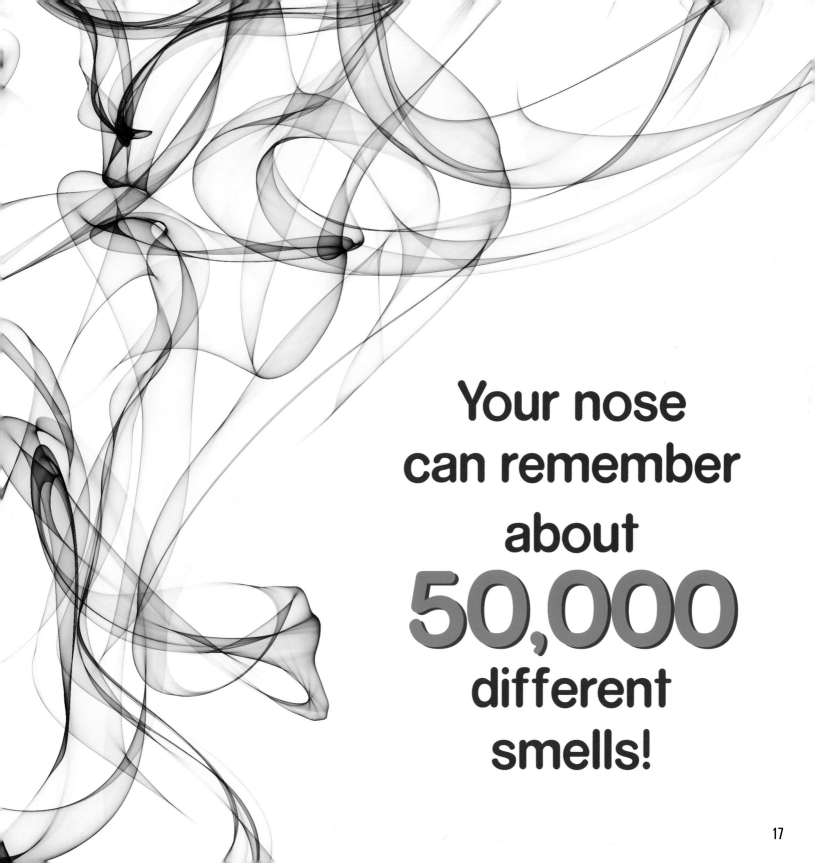

Your nose
can remember
about
50,000
different
smells!

It takes about **12 HOURS** to completely digest eaten FOOD.

YOUR EYES STAY THE SAME SIZE AS THE DAY YOU WERE BORN.

A pair of feet have **500,000 SWEAT GLANDS** and can produce more than a **pint** of SWEAT a day.

INFANTS only BLINK about ONCE a MINUTE.

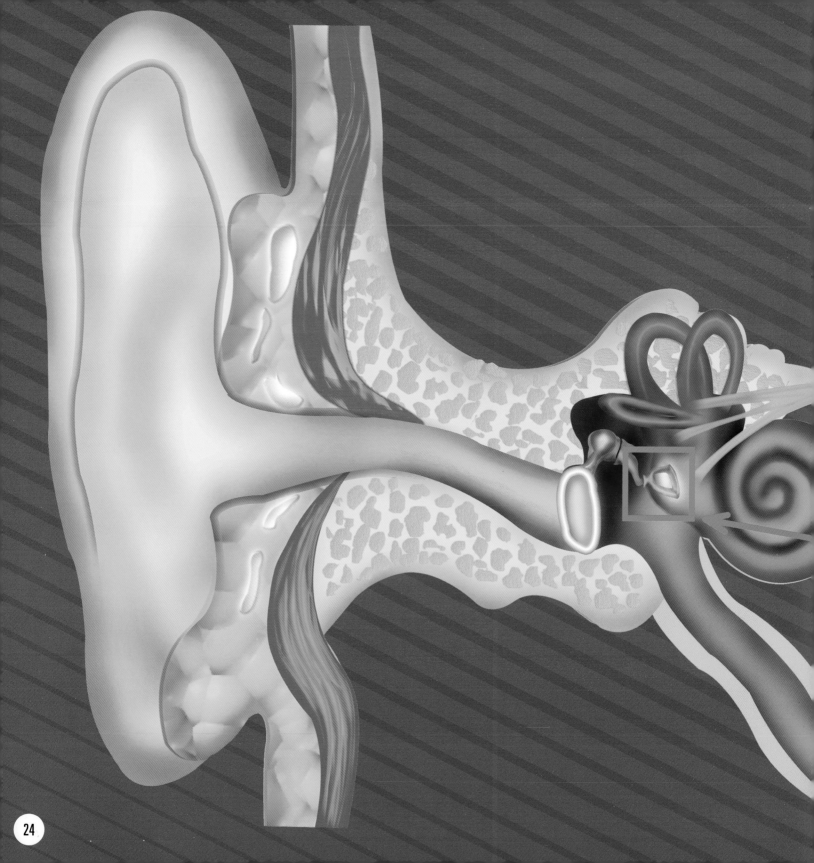

THE SMALLEST BONE IN YOUR BODY IS INSIDE YOUR EAR.

IT'S CALLED A STIRRUP AND IT'S ABOUT THE SIZE OF A GRAIN OF RICE.

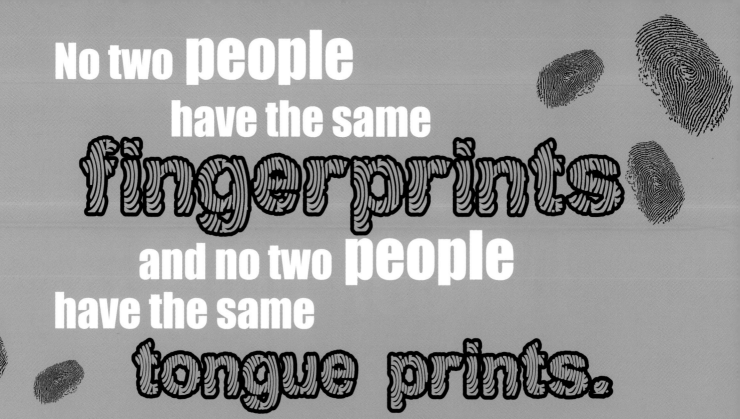

No two **people** have the same **fingerprints** and no two **people** have the same **tongue prints.**

Women have stronger senses of smell than men.

Women
and
children
breathe
faster than
men.

PEOPLE WHO **DAYDREAM** ARE MORE LIKELY TO REMEMBER THEIR NIGHTTIME DREAMS.

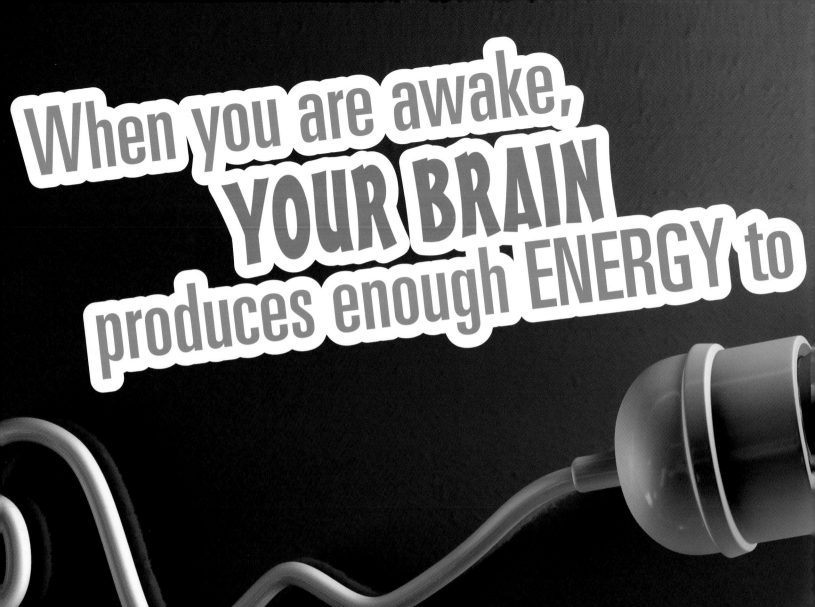

When you are awake,
YOUR BRAIN
produces enough ENERGY to

LIGHT UP

a small LIGHT BULB.

POOL x 2

During your life, you will produce enough spit to fill two SWIMMING POOLS.

ABOUT 1 IN EVERY 2,000 BABIES ARE BORN WITH TEETH.

THE PUPILS IN YOUR EYES CAN BECOME BIGGER WHEN YOU HEAR NOISE.

Babies cannot see COLORS when they're born. They can only see

BLACK
&
WHITE.

Healthy food helps your body work right—like gas makes a car go.

Your brain controls everything you do.

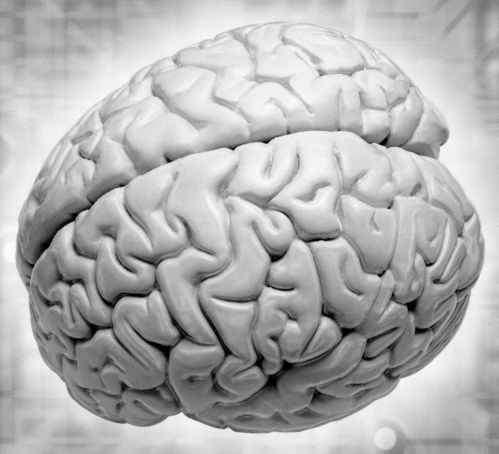

It's like your own personal computer.

Exercise can make you smarter

because more blood flows to your **brain.**

THE **OLDER** YOU ARE, THE MORE LIKELY YOU ARE TO HAVE MITES—TINY BUGS THAT ARE IMPOSSIBLE TO SEE WITHOUT A MICROSCOPE—LIVING ON YOUR EYELASHES.

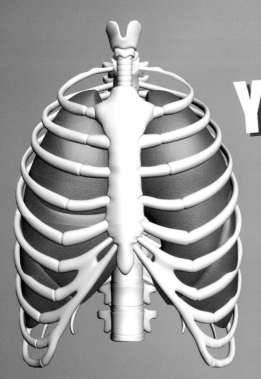

Your lungs are [protected] by your rib cage.

More people have brown eyes than any other color.

SKIN IS THE BODY'S BIGGEST ORGAN.

A cool room may help you SLEEP ZZzz better.

WHEN A PERSON TELLS A **LIE**, HIS OR HER **NOSE** AND THE AREA AROUND THE **EYES** BECOME **WARMER**.

SUGAR can make you feel HUNGRY.

Eating sugar can also make you feel **tired** and **lazy**.

Eating too much sugar messes with the **signals** that your brain sends to tell your **stomach** it's full.

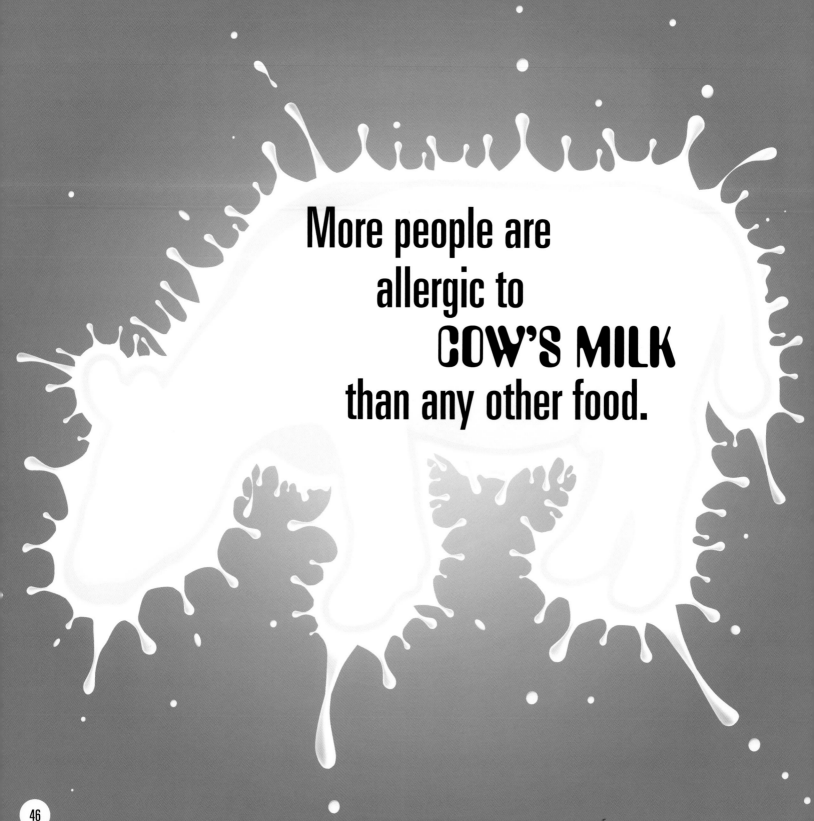

More people are
allergic to
COW'S MILK
than any other food.

Children are more sensitive to DIFFERENT TASTES than adults.

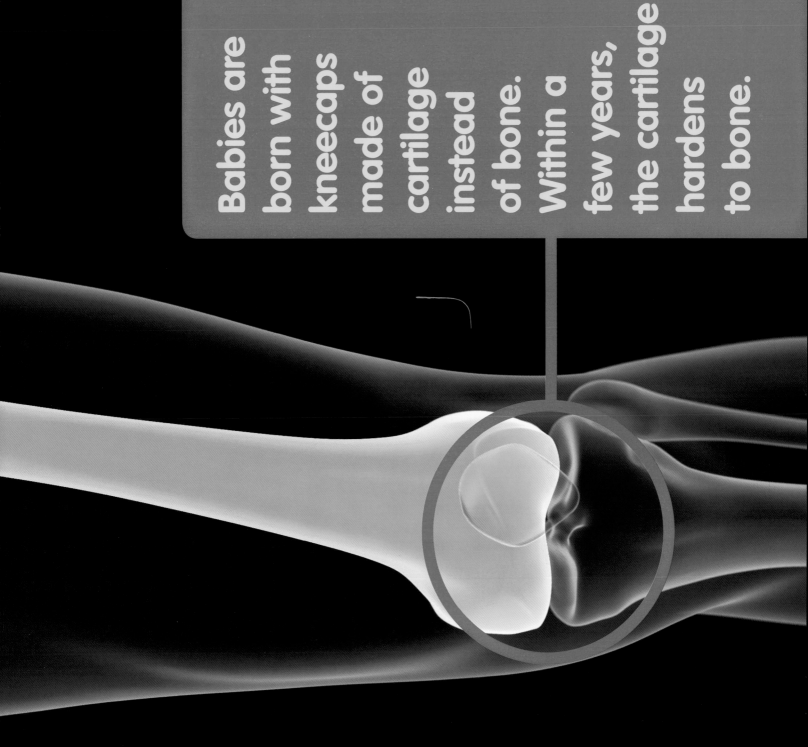

Babies are born with kneecaps made of cartilage instead of bone. Within a few years, the cartilage hardens to bone.

NEWBORNS MAKE NOISE TO CRY, BUT THEY DON'T SHED TEARS.

TEARS AREN'T MADE UNTIL THEY ARE ONE TO THREE MONTHS OLD.

THE BRAIN CAN STAY ALIVE FOR THREE TO FIVE MINUTES WITHOUT OXYGEN.

You get a new **STOMACH LINING** every three to four days. If you didn't, the **ACIDS** in your tummy would **DIGEST** your stomach, and you'd basically be **EATING** yourself!

YOUR **HEARTBEAT** CAN CHANGE TO MIMIC THE MUSIC YOU ARE LISTENING TO.

THERE ARE 150 BILLION RED BLOOD CELLS IN ONE OUNCE OF BLOOD.

The **surface area** of a lung could cover

ONE SIDE (HALF) of a tennis court.

SPECIAL **CELLS** IN YOUR **SKIN** PRODUCE **VITAMIN D** WHEN YOUR **BODY** IS EXPOSED TO **SUNLIGHT.**

CHILDREN GROW *FASTER* IN THE SPRING.

As a kid, your HEART is about the same size as your FIST.

THE EYE CAN DISTINGUISH ABOUT 10 MILLION DIFFERENT COLORS.

RED BLOOD CELLS
MOVE THROUGH YOUR ENTIRE BODY IN ABOUT
20 SECONDS.

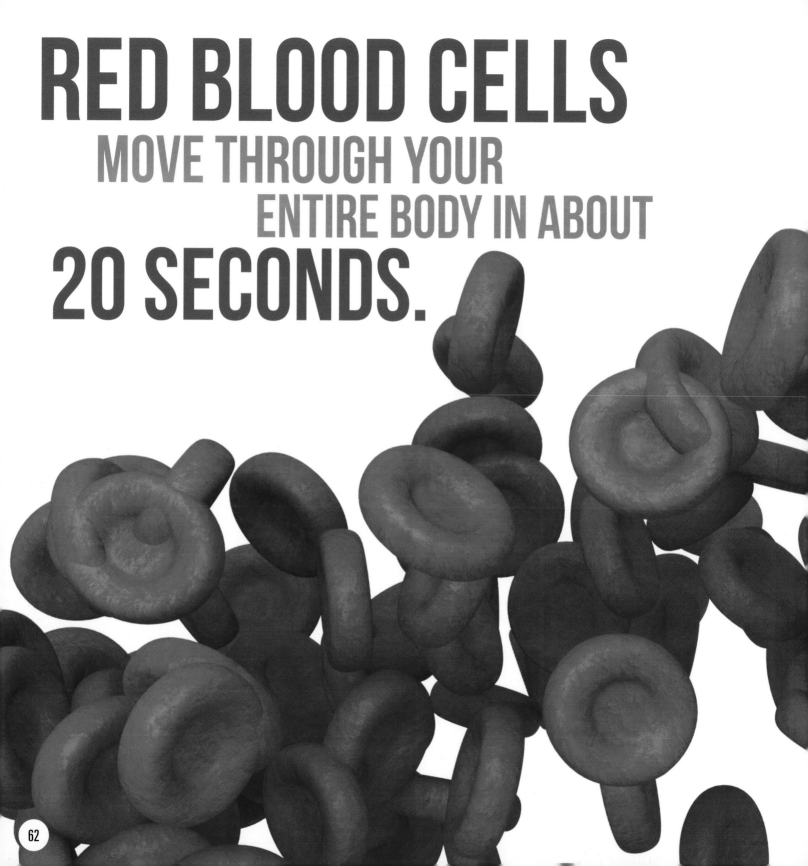

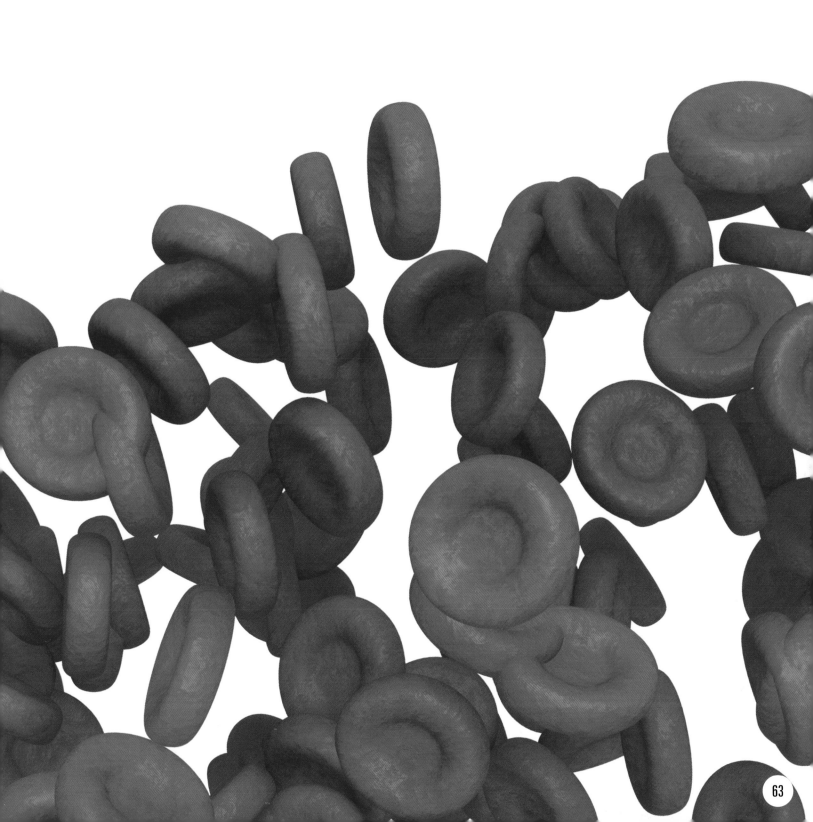

YOU LOSE ABOUT HALF YOUR TASTE BUDS BY AGE 60.

GOOSEBUMPS

are caused by **MUSCLES** attached to **HAIR FOLLICLES.**

They **LITERALLY** make our hair **STAND UP!**

The
average
**human
head**
has about
**100,000
hairs.**

HUMANS ARE NOT THE ONLY PRIMATES POSSESSING OPPOSABLE THUMBS.

OPPOSABLE
MEANS THAT THUMBS CAN MOVE TOWARDS YOUR FINGERS AND HELP THEM TO DO THEIR WORK.

ABOUT

⅓ OF THE

HUMAN RACE

HAS PERFECT,

OR 20-20,

VISION.

A FULL BLADDER is about the size of a SOFTBALL.

IN ONE MONTH, YOU WILL HAVE A COMPLETELY DIFFERENT TOP LAYER OF SKIN THAN YOU HAVE NOW.

AS AN ADULT, YOUR BRAIN WEIGHS ABOUT THE SAME AS THREE FOOTBALLS.

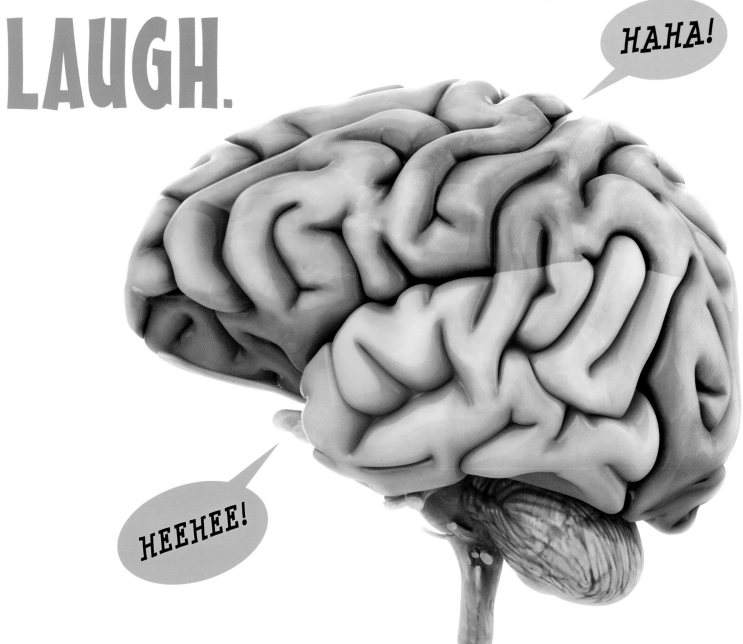

THE HIGHEST BODY TEMPERATURE EVER RECORDED WAS A

FEVER OF 115.7 DEGREES FAHRENHEIT.

The **average person** goes to the **bathroom**

6 times a day.

All together, the **DIGESTIVE ORGANS** are **30 FEET LONG.**

BELLY BUTTONS are actually **SCARS** created when

your **UMBILICAL CORD** was **CUT.**

10%

OF PEOPLE ARE LEFT-HANDED.

As you age, the connective tissue and collagen in your face isn't as strong or supportive as it used to be. This causes wrinkles.

A healthy **LIVER** can constantly **REGENERATE** itself—which means if **part of the liver** is donated, it will **GROW BACK!**

Unless you have an IDENTICAL TWIN, the way YOU look is UNIQUE!

According to **GERMAN** fairy tales, meeting your "doppelganger," or "double-goer," is very **BAD LUCK.**

After **DONATING BLOOD,** your body takes only 24 **HOURS** to **REPLACE PLASMA** but **4 TO 6 WEEKS** to replace **RED BLOOD CELLS.**

If a scientist had a strand of human hair, he or she couldn't tell if it came from a male or female.

COUGHING CAN CAUSE AIR TO MOVE THROUGH YOUR WINDPIPE *FASTER* THAN THE SPEED OF SOUND — OVER **1,000** FEET PER SECOND!

THE BEST WAY TO PREVENT GETTING SICK IS WASHING YOUR HANDS.

There are **EIGHT** bones in the wrist.

BESIDES PEOPLE, KOALAS, CHIMPS, AND GORILLAS ARE THE ONLY OTHER LIVING THINGS THAT HAVE FINGERPRINTS.

Brushing your teeth twice every day can keep your heart healthy!

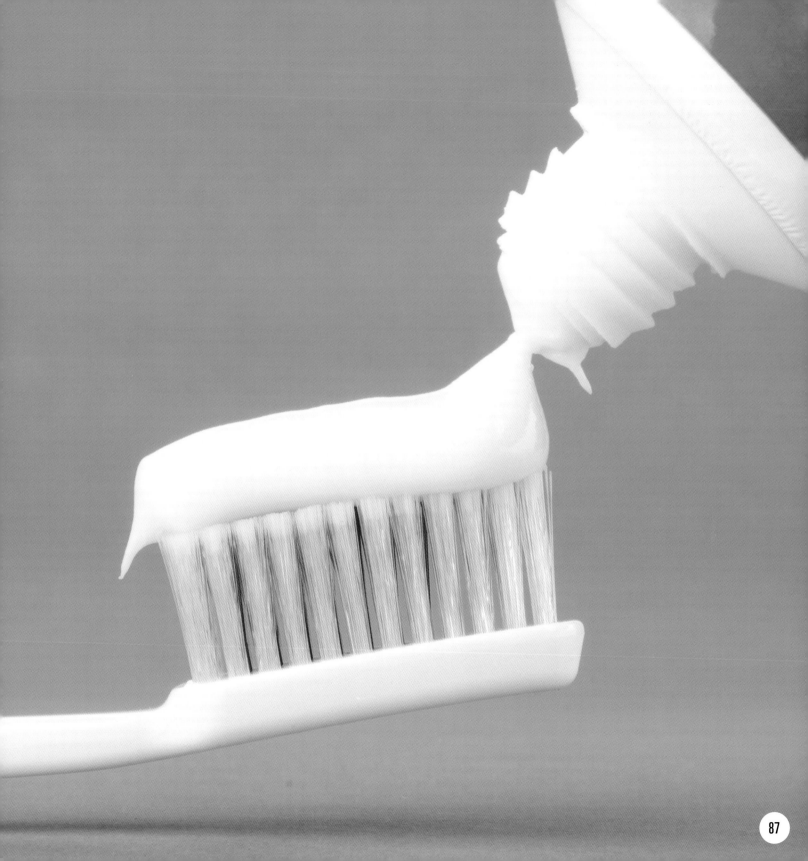

If your tongue is **DRY**, you can't taste.

You need **SALIVA** to **DISSOLVE** food in order to taste it.

There are 14 BONES and over 40 MUSCLES in your face.

When typing, the average person uses the LEFT hand ← more than → *the RIGHT.*

THERE ARE 206 BONES IN YOUR BODY. WITHOUT THEM YOU WOULD BE A SHAPELESS BLOB!

There is no hair on your palms.

The muscles that move your fingers are in your palms.

The **largest muscle** in your body is your rear end, also known as **gluteus maximus.**

A BLINK USUALLY LASTS 100 TO 150 MILLISECONDS, MEANING YOU CAN BLINK FIVE TIMES IN A SECOND.

The width of your arm span is about the same as the length of your body.

KIDS AND GROWNUPS

GET ABOUT SEVEN

COLDS PER YEAR.

ON AVERAGE, WE DRINK ABOUT 16,000 GALLONS OF WATER IN A LIFETIME.

If you lose a **FINGERNAIL,** it will take about **SIX MONTHS** to grow a **NEW ONE.**

LAUGHING can help keep your ♥ HEART ♥ healthy!

THERE ARE ABOUT 9,000 TASTE BUDS ON YOUR TONGUE, IN YOUR THROAT, AND ON THE ROOF OF YOUR MOUTH.

THE HUMAN HEART CAN CONTINUE TO BEAT WHEN IT IS REMOVED FROM THE BODY, AS LONG AS IT HAS AN ADEQUATE SUPPLY OF OXYGEN.

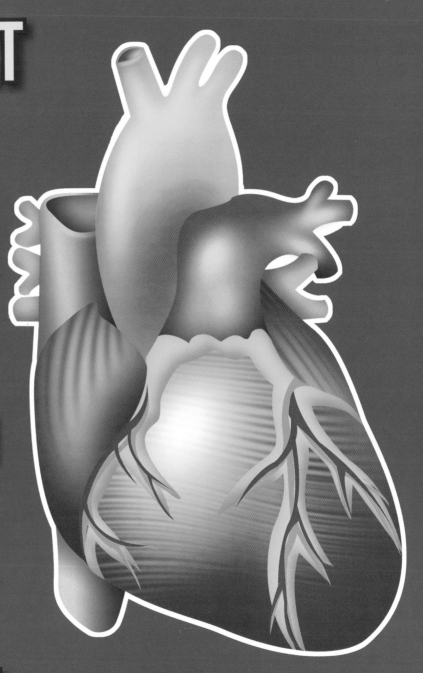

Fingernails grow about one-tenth of an inch each month.

BY 60 YEARS OF AGE, 60% OF MEN AND 40% OF WOMEN WILL SNORE.

Blinking helps keep your eyeballs clean and moist.

THE HEART

weighs
between
7 and 15 ounces,
about the same
weight as a
bottle of
ketchup.

On average, babies start smiling at about 12 weeks of age.

In the span of 24 hours, you will take about 23,000 breaths.

WE START TO GRADUALLY SHRINK FROM THE TIME WE'RE 30 YEARS OLD ON.

Every person, **except** identical twins, has a completely **unique** smell.

103

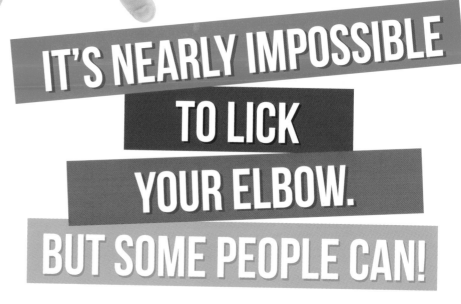

IT'S NEARLY IMPOSSIBLE TO LICK YOUR ELBOW. BUT SOME PEOPLE CAN!

YOU SHOULD DRINK **TWO LITERS,** OR **ABOUT** HALF A GALLON, OF WATER PER **DAY.**

IT'S NEARLY IMPOSSIBLE TO TICKLE YOURSELF. YOUR BRAIN KNOWS YOUR TOUCH FROM SOMEBODY ELSE'S.

BRAIN CELLS CANNOT REGENERATE.

HUMAN BONES ARE STRONGER THAN STEEL.

Injuries to the surface of eyes (like scratches) heal very fast—usually in about two to three days.

A HICCUP IS AN INVOLUNTARY SPASM OF THE DIAPHRAGM.

YOU CAN HICCUP ANYWHERE FROM 4 TO 60 TIMES PER MINUTE!

When you eat, drink or swallow spit, you also swallow a little air. When you digest food, gas builds up in your body and makes you burp or fart!

Eyebrows help keep water and sweat out of our eyes.

The
human body
produces about
a liter of
mucus per
day.

Together, all of the bacteria in one body weighs about four pounds.

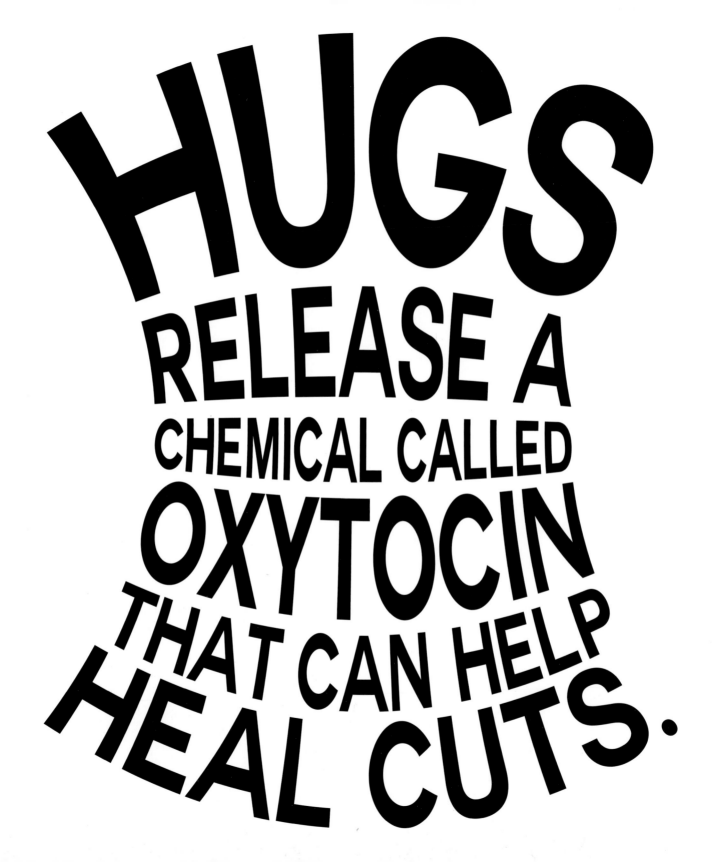

HUGS RELEASE A CHEMICAL CALLED OXYTOCIN THAT CAN HELP HEAL CUTS.

The feet of babies don't have arches.
Arches usually appear when a child is around two.

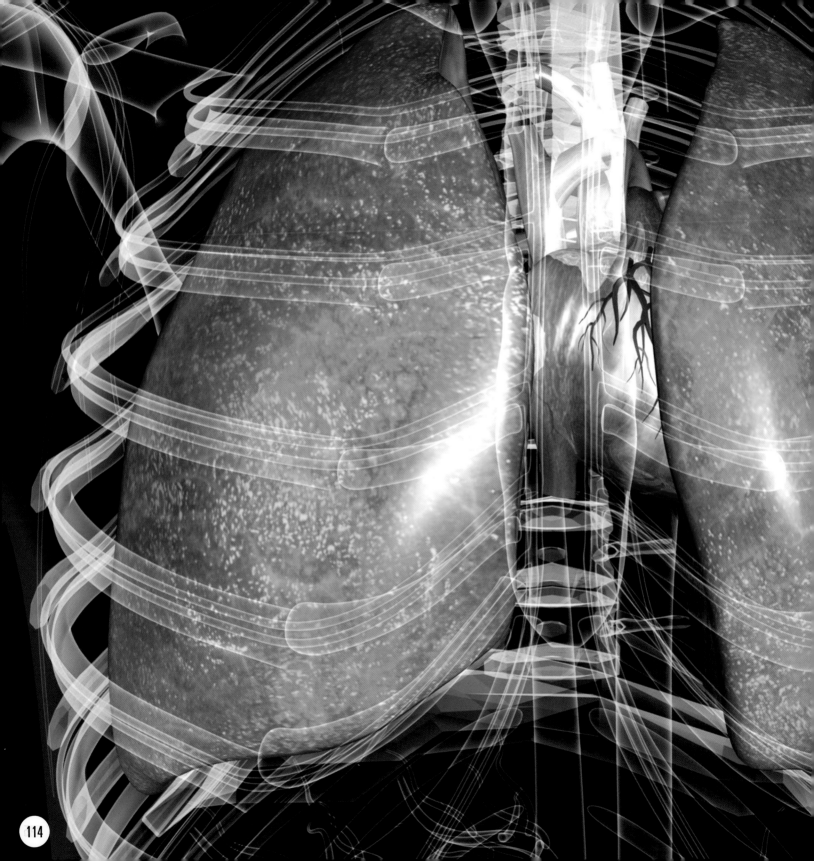

Most people are able to read 250 words per minute.

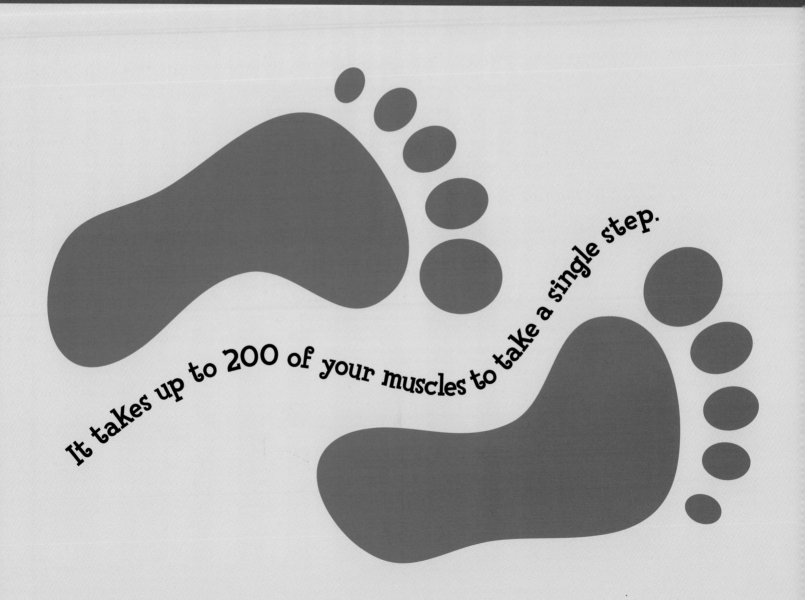

It takes up to 200 of your muscles to take a single step.

We have **50 percent** of the same **DNA** as a

banana.

EATING TOO MANY CARROTS CAN CAUSE YOUR SKIN TO TURN ORANGE.

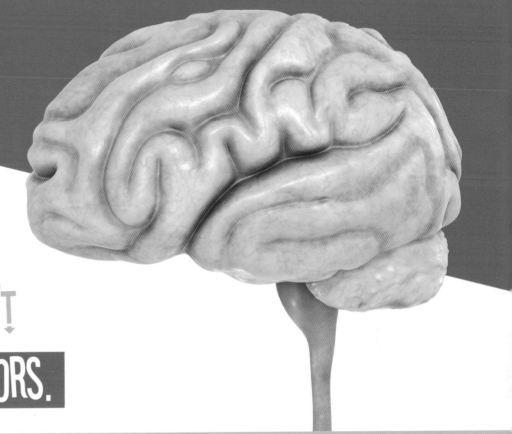

YOUR BRAIN CAN FEEL NO PAIN BECAUSE IT DOESN'T HAVE PAIN RECEPTORS.

AN ADULT'S HEART IS ABOUT THE SIZE OF A GRAPEFRUIT.

RIDING A BIKE, RUNNING, PLAYING— OR ANY KIND OF EXERCISE— MAKES YOUR HEART HEALTHY AND HAPPY!

YOUR BODY ACTS LIKE A TRASH CAN THAT IS FULL. YOU MUST EMPTY IT (PEE AND POOP) EVERY DAY TO KEEP IT HEALTHY.

Most people have about **four dreams** every night.

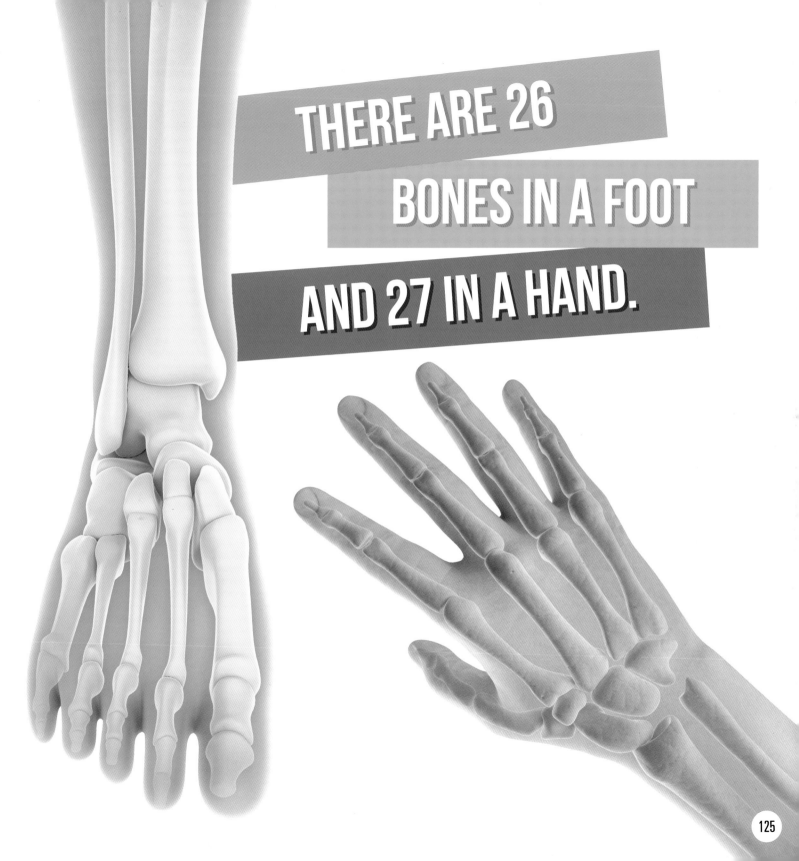

THERE ARE 26 BONES IN A FOOT AND 27 IN A HAND.

THE BONES IN YOUR BODY ARE AS STRONG AS A PIECE OF GRANITE.

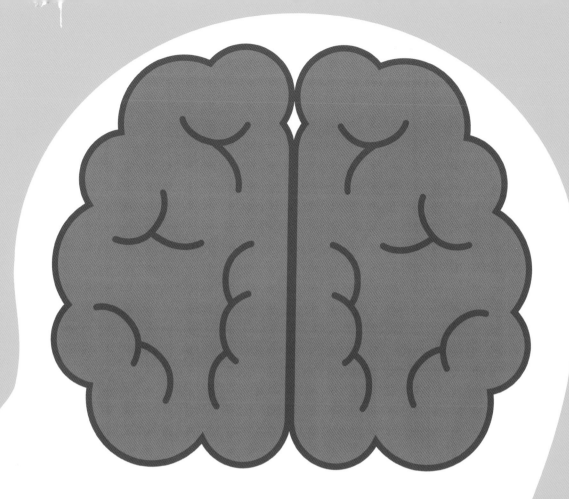

Your brain is the **fattest** organ in your body.

SNOT

IS MADE OF **WATER** AS WELL AS TINY PARTICLES THAT ARE IN THE AIR WE BREATHE LIKE **GERMS, DUST** AND **POLLEN.**

WHEN
ALL THAT
DRIES OUT,
IT
TURNS INTO A
BOOGER.

You are TALLER in the MORNING than at NIGHT.

THE AVERAGE HEAD

In 30 minutes, the human body produces enough heat to boil a half gallon of water.

WEIGHS 10 POUNDS.

A CATERPILLAR HAS MORE MUSCLES THAN A HUMAN BODY.

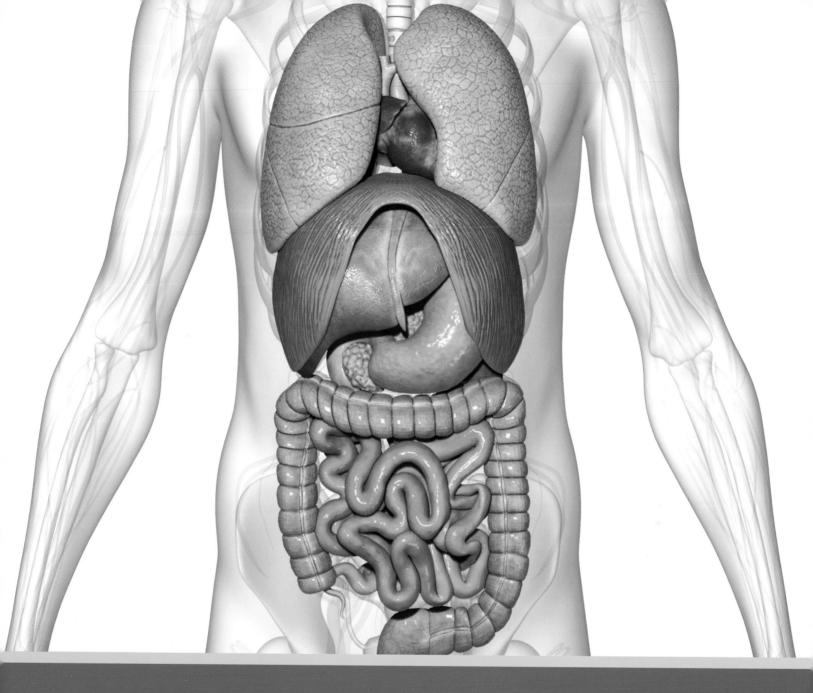

YOU HAVE 22 INTERNAL ORGANS.

THE INABILITY TO SEE IS CALLED BLINDNESS.

THE INABILITY TO HEAR IS CALLED DEAFNESS.

MOST CAUCASIAN BABIES ARE BORN WITH BLUE EYES.

HAIR GROWTH is defined by GENETICS.

Every day, we lose about 50 to 100 hairs.

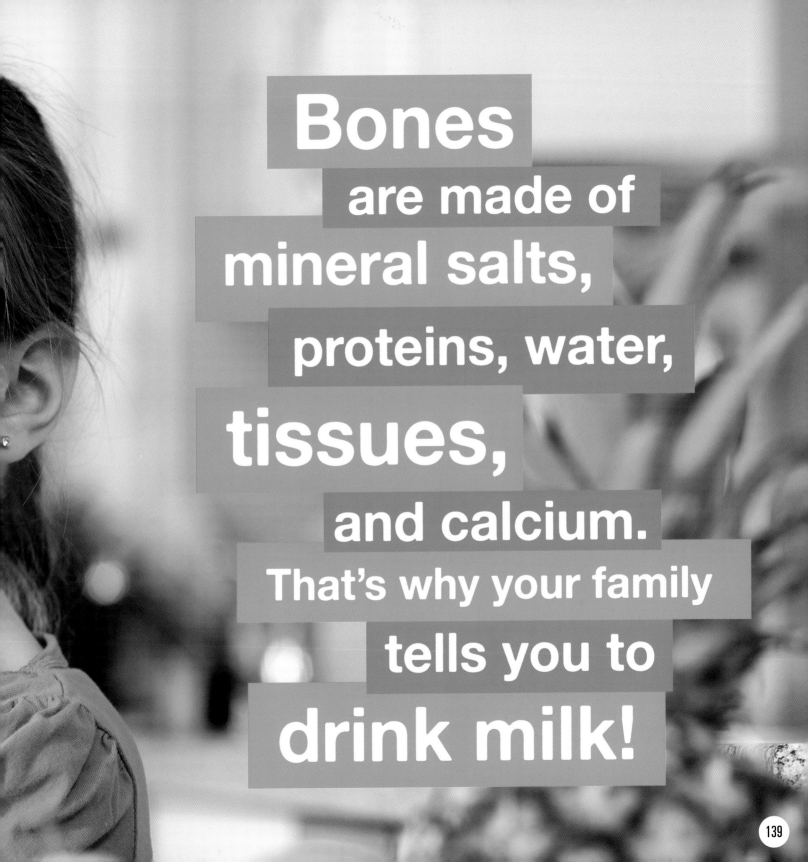

Bones are made of mineral salts, proteins, water, **tissues,** and calcium. That's why your family tells you to **drink milk!**

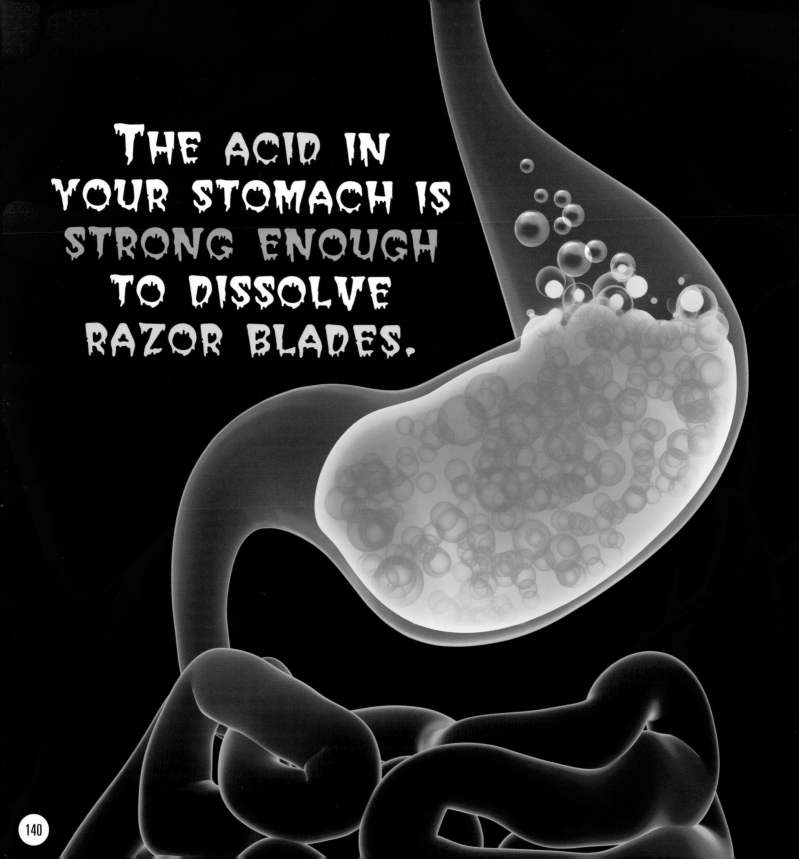

THE ACID IN YOUR STOMACH IS STRONG ENOUGH TO DISSOLVE RAZOR BLADES.

YOUR BLOOD **TRAVELS** THROUGH YOUR VESSELS **12,000** *MILES* IN ONE DAY.

THAT WOULD BE LIKE TRAVELING FROM **NEW YORK** TO *CALIFORNIA* FOUR TIMES.

Most of the dust found in your house is dead skin that has been shed.

Children generally have a better sense of smell than adults.

The speed of a **Cheetahs,** is about **100** the fastest land animals, **60 miles**

sneeze
miles per hour.
can run at only
per hour!

THE
MOST
COMMON
BLOOD
TYPE IS
O POSITIVE.

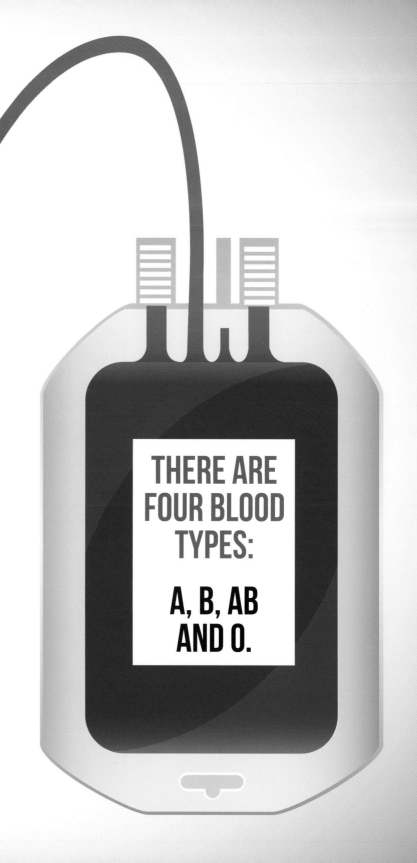

THERE ARE
FOUR BLOOD
TYPES:

A, B, AB
AND O.

WHITE BLOOD CELLS MAKE UP ABOUT 1% OF BLOOD.

The bacteria in your belly button is unique to you.

The average growth of hair is half an inch per month.

In your lifetime, your heart will pump about 200 train tank cars full of blood.

You have a bone at the base of your tongue.

It is the only bone in your body that is not connected to another.

BLUE-EYED PEOPLE SHARE A COMMON ANCESTOR WITH EVERY OTHER BLUE-EYED PERSON IN THE WORLD.

It is impossible to **SWALLOW** and **BREATHE** at the SAME TIME.

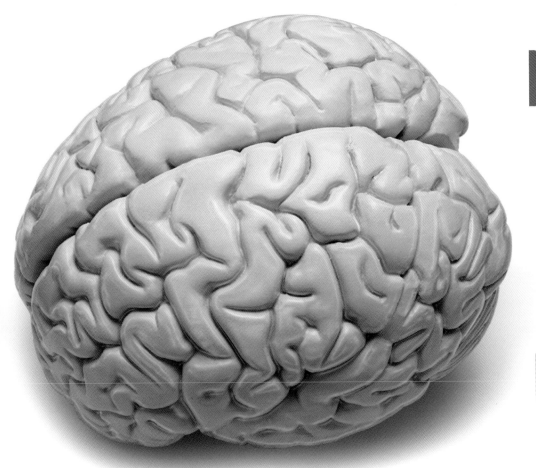

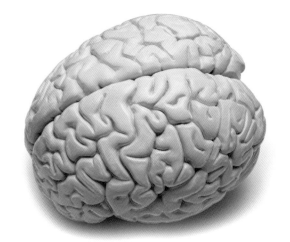

The **human** brain is **two** to **three** times as **big** as the **brain** of other **mammals** that are of a **similar** body size.

DREAMS may last anywhere from **FIVE** to **FORTY-FIVE** minutes.

If you NEVER cut your hair, it could GROW up to 5 feet long!

THE LONGEST PREGNANCY ON RECORD WAS 12½ MONTHS.

85% of people can curl their tongue. Can you?

Your brain is a wrinkly, pink organ that feels a bit like a soft mushroom.

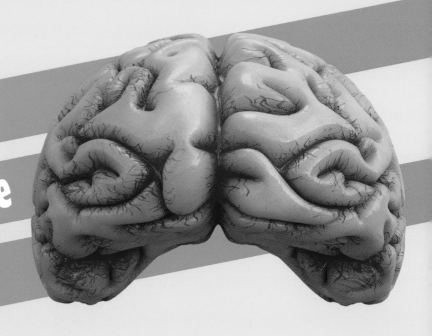

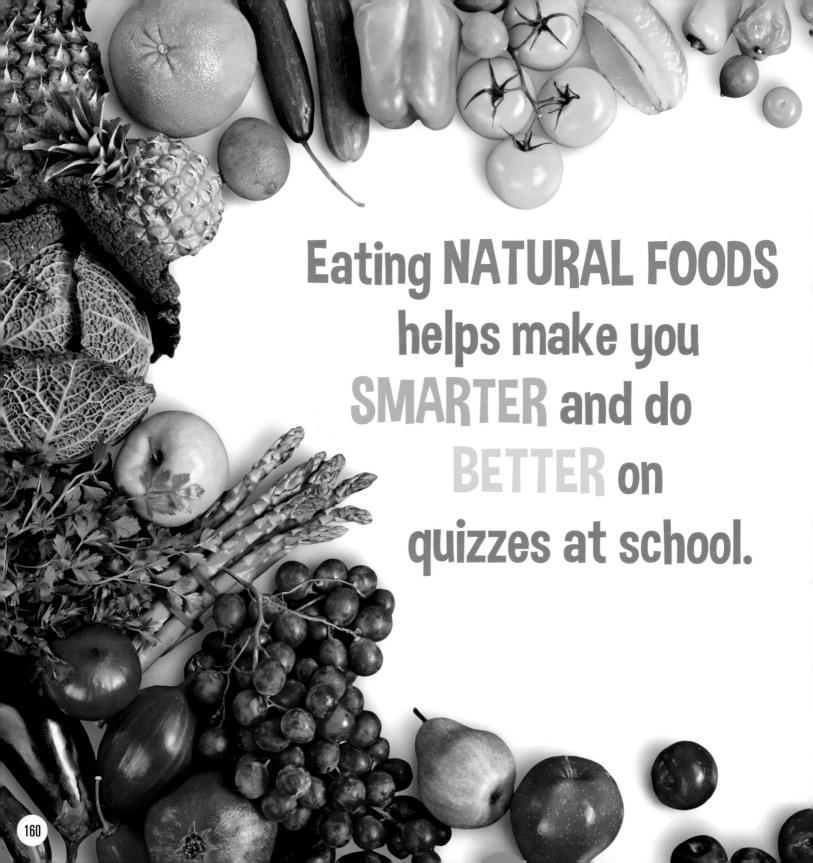

Eating **NATURAL FOODS** helps make you **SMARTER** and do **BETTER** on quizzes at school.

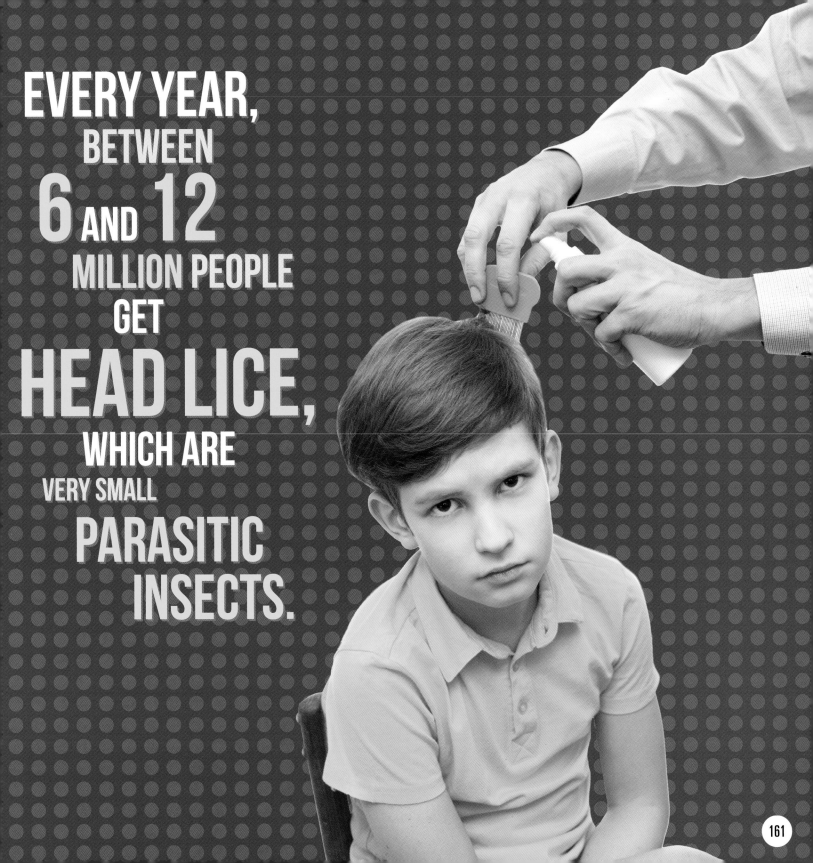

EVERY YEAR, BETWEEN 6 AND 12 MILLION PEOPLE GET HEAD LICE, WHICH ARE VERY SMALL PARASITIC INSECTS.

THE SMELL OF CHOCOLATE INCREASES CERTAIN BRAIN WAVES THAT HELP RELAX YOU.

YOUR BRAIN IS MADE UP OF 80 PERCENT WATER.

Not all GERMS are bad. There are BACTERIA in your stomach that help you DIGEST food, and bacteria on your skin that allow blood to CLOT when you are cut.

Air passing through your **NOSE** is warmed to match your **BODY TEMPERATURE,** or it is cooled if it is very hot.

YOUR SKIN WEIGHS *TWICE* AS MUCH AS **YOUR BRAIN.**

Blood **PUMPS** through the **AORTA** at **ONE** mile per hour.

SPEED LIMIT 1

Exercise helps make you smarter and happier.

Doctors recommend getting
at least a half hour per day.

It is believed some people dream in BLACK and WHITE.

Your thigh bone is HOLLOW!

You have about **70,000** thoughts per day. That's almost **49 thoughts** per minute!

THE SOUND YOU HEAR WHEN YOU LISTEN TO A HEARTBEAT IS FROM THE FOUR HEART VALVES CLOSING.

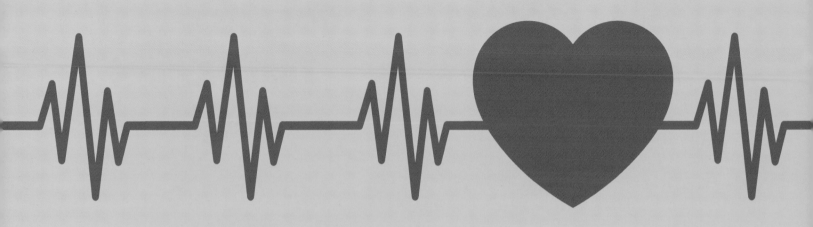

Older people have GRAY HAIR because the cells that control hair color DIE AS YOU AGE.

LAUGHTER is contagious.

BAD BREATH

is caused by anything from NOT brushing your TEETH to certain MEDICAL conditions.

About 3 million kids in the United States are allergic to nuts, seafood, milk, eggs, soy, or wheat.

FOOD
STAYS IN YOUR
STOMACH
FOR TWO
TO FOUR
HOURS.

The part of your brain called the **HIPPOCAMPUS** is responsible for memory.

It grows **LARGER** as you memorize more things.

BONE MARROW is sort of like a **THICK JELLY;** it makes **BLOOD CELLS.**

HAVING NO SENSE OF TASTE IS CALLED AGEUSIA.

YOUR
FOREARM
(FROM THE INSIDE OF YOUR ELBOW TO THE INSIDE OF YOUR WRIST)

IS THE
SAME LENGTH
AS YOUR
FOOT.

BOTH
BOYS AND **GIRLS**
EXPERIENCE
VOICE CHANGES
AS THEY GROW **OLDER.**

About **75 percent** of **POOP** is **WATER** and the rest is **GERMS** and undigested **PLANT FIBERS.**

NOSE BLEEDS can be caused by nose picking, allergies, a cold, and indoor dry heated air.

YOUR MOUTH USES 75 MUSCLES TO HELP YOU SPEAK.

The **RIGHT SIDE** of your **BRAIN** tells the **LEFT SIDE** of your **BODY** what to do,

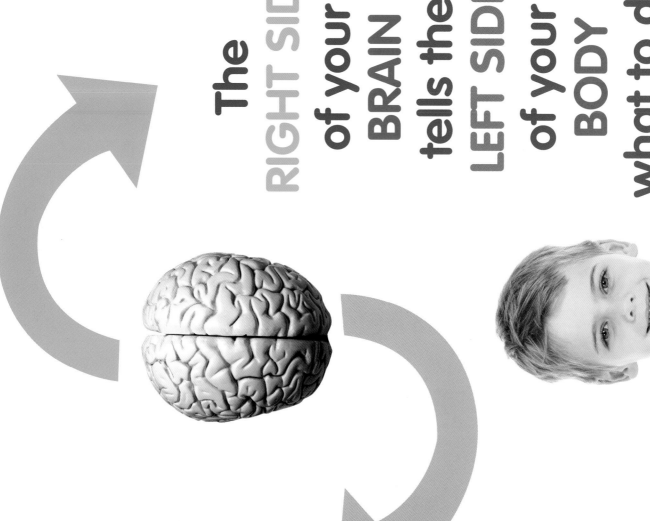

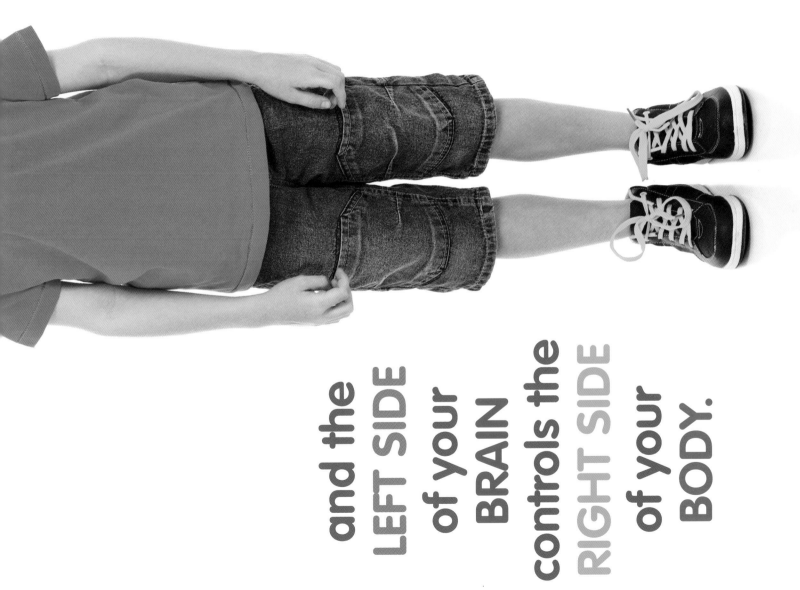

and the
LEFT SIDE
of your
BRAIN
controls the
RIGHT SIDE
of your
BODY.

There is fluid surrounding your brain that protects it from bumps or knocks, and also any illness.

Some people are born with ....·٠ two different colored eyes.

The nail on your middle finger grows faster than the nails on your other fingers.

Facial hair grows FASTER than any other body hair. If a man didn't trim or shave his BEARD it could GROW to be over 30 feet long!

Having a FEVER is a good thing—it's your body's way of fighting off SICKNESS.

WOMEN'S HANDS AND FEET GET COLDER THAN MEN'S.

ONLY HUMANS CRY TEARS WHEN THEY ARE SAD OR HAPPY.

THE
TECHNICAL
TERM FOR
SMELLING IS
OLFACTION.

ANOSMIA
IS THE
INABILITY
TO SMELL.

A newborn BABY only has about one cup of blood in his or her body.

The **MUSCLES** in your **EYES** are more **ACTIVE** than **ANY** other **MUSCLES** in your **BODY.**

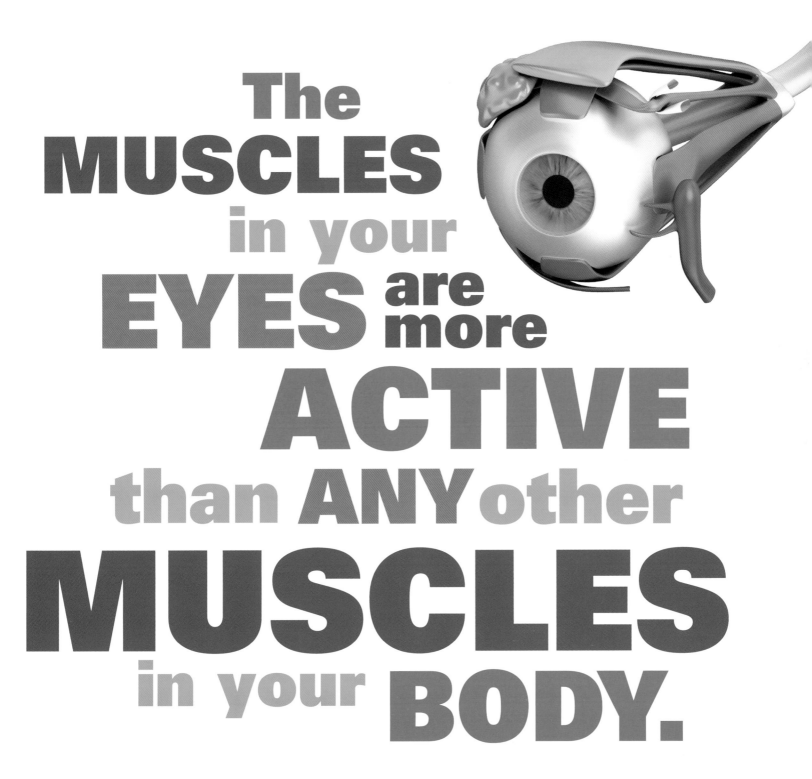

Most people read slower on a

computer than they do a book.

When you BLUSH, the lining of your STOMACH blushes, too.

BLOOD MAKES A FULL CIRCUIT OF THE BODY IN ABOUT ONE MINUTE.

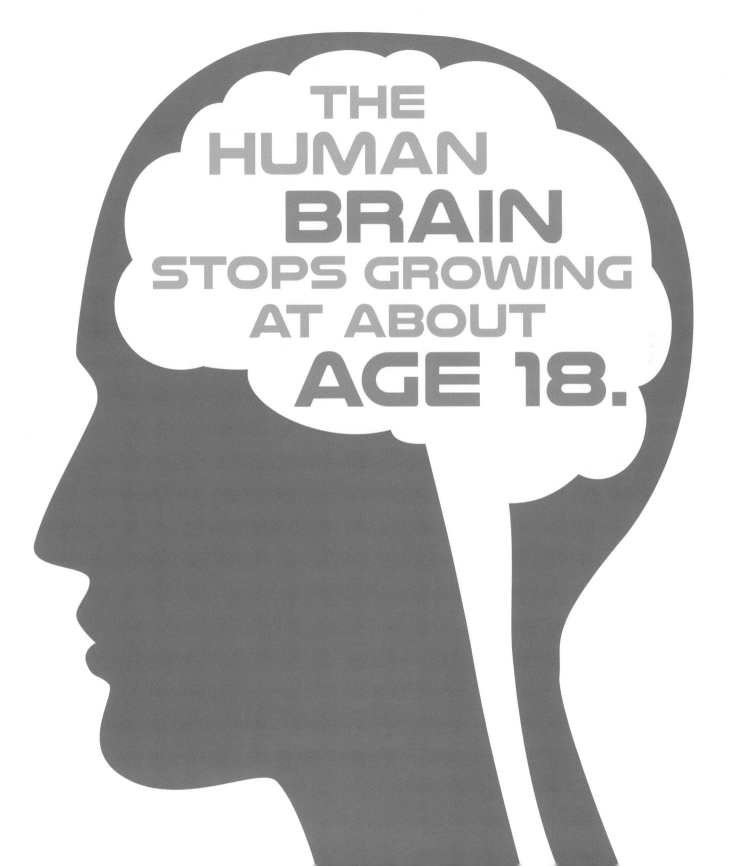

It is possible to live with only one lung and one kidney.

Getting frequent trims does not make your hair grow faster.

198

HUMANS SHED ABOUT 600,000 PARTICLES OF SKIN EVERY HOUR. THAT WORKS OUT TO BE ABOUT 1.6 POUNDS OF SKIN EACH YEAR.

A **kitchen faucet** would have to be turned on *all the way* and run for at least **45 years** to pump the amount of **blood pumped** in an *average lifetime.*

THE EARS AND THE END OF THE NOSE DO NOT HAVE BONES IN THEM.

Most people BLINK about 12 times a minute.

The tooth is the only part of the human body that cannot heal.

THE SPLEEN HELPS FILTER OUT OLD RED BLOOD CELLS AND OTHER IMPURITIES IN THE BLOOD, WHILE ALSO BEING THE STORAGE SPACE FOR WHITE BLOOD CELLS AND PLATELETS.

THE AVERAGE HEIGHT OF AN ADULT HUMAN IS ABOUT 5 TO 6 FEET TALL.

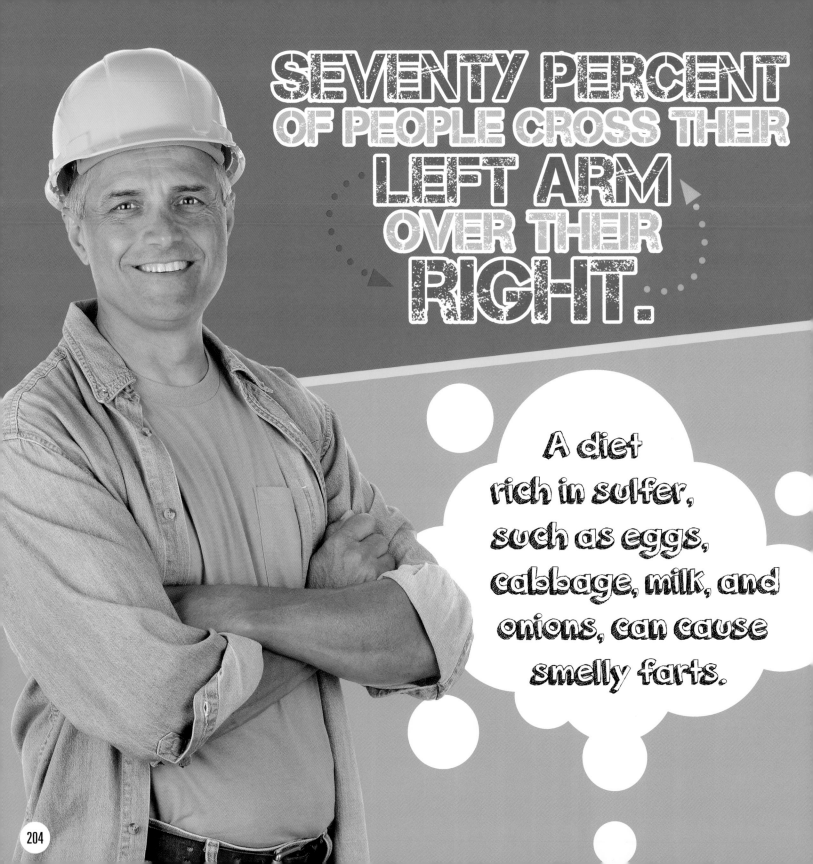

The diaphragm is a **long muscle** beneath the lungs that ***contracts*** in and out, causing you to breathe.

YOUR NERVOUS SYSTEM TRANSMITS MESSAGES TO YOUR BRAIN

AT A SPEED OF ABOUT 180 MILES PER HOUR!

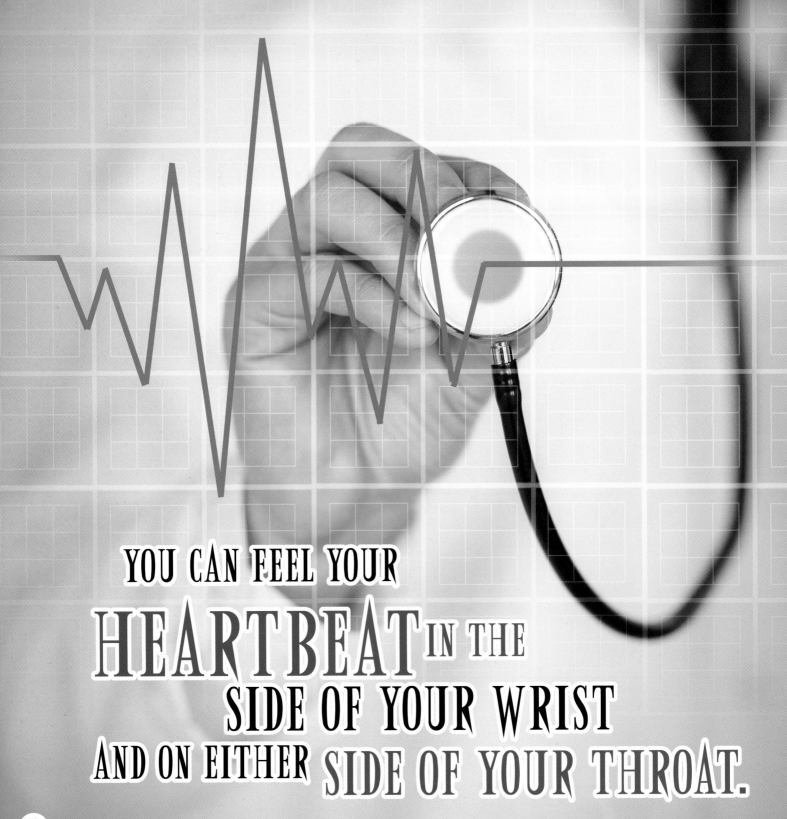

YOU CAN FEEL YOUR **HEARTBEAT** IN THE SIDE OF YOUR WRIST AND ON EITHER SIDE OF YOUR THROAT.

Muscle tissue is denser than fatty tissue.

THE TONGUE IS MADE UP OF EIGHT DIFFERENT MUSCLES.

NOSE HAIRS ARE IMPORTANT! THEY HELP FILTER OUT DUST AND OTHER DEBRIS WHEN YOU BREATHE.

If all the blood body were laid a total length of about that's long enough world vessels in a human out they would have 60,000 miles; to circle the two and a half times!

YOUR FUNNY BONE IS ACTUALLY A NERVE, CALLED THE ULNAR NERVE. IT GETS ITS NICKNAME FROM THE WEIRD TINGLE CAUSED BY HITTING IT.

WHEN YOU ARE EMBARRASSED, YOUR BODY RELEASES ADRENALINE, CAUSING YOU TO BLUSH. NERVES AT THE BASE OF YOUR SPINE CONTROL BLUSHING.

Most females are capable of giving birth to **35** children in a lifetime.

PEOPLE HAVE BEEN PIERCING THEIR EARS FOR THOUSANDS OF YEARS.

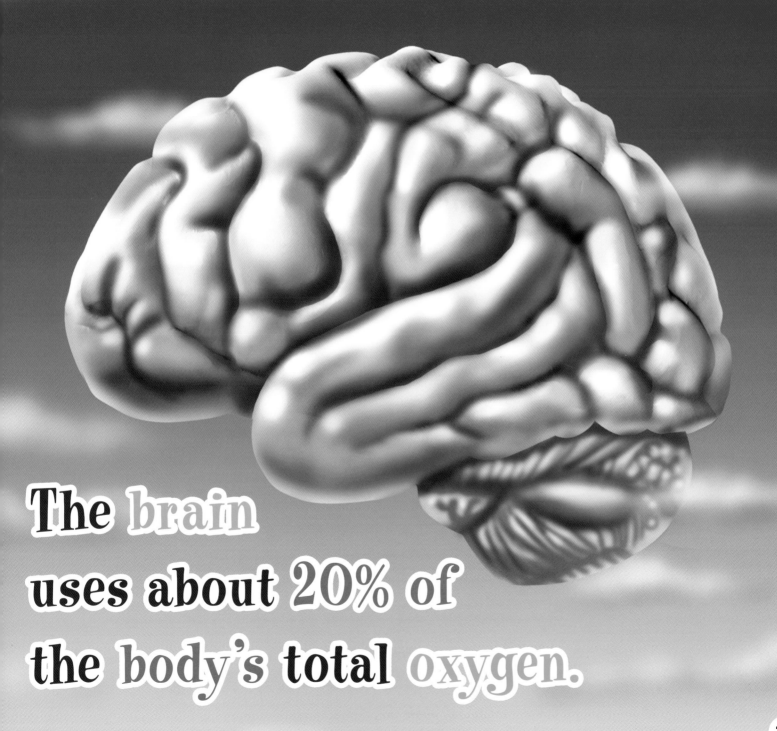

The brain uses about 20% of the body's total oxygen.

MEN and **WOMEN** get HICCUPS with the same **FREQUENCY.**

But **MEN** tend to have more **PERSISTENT** hiccups, which can last for **MORE THAN TWO DAYS.**

EVERYBODY FEELS SHY AT TIMES, EVEN GROWNUPS.

The **heart** *pumps* about 2,000 gallons of blood *through* *blood vessels* every day.

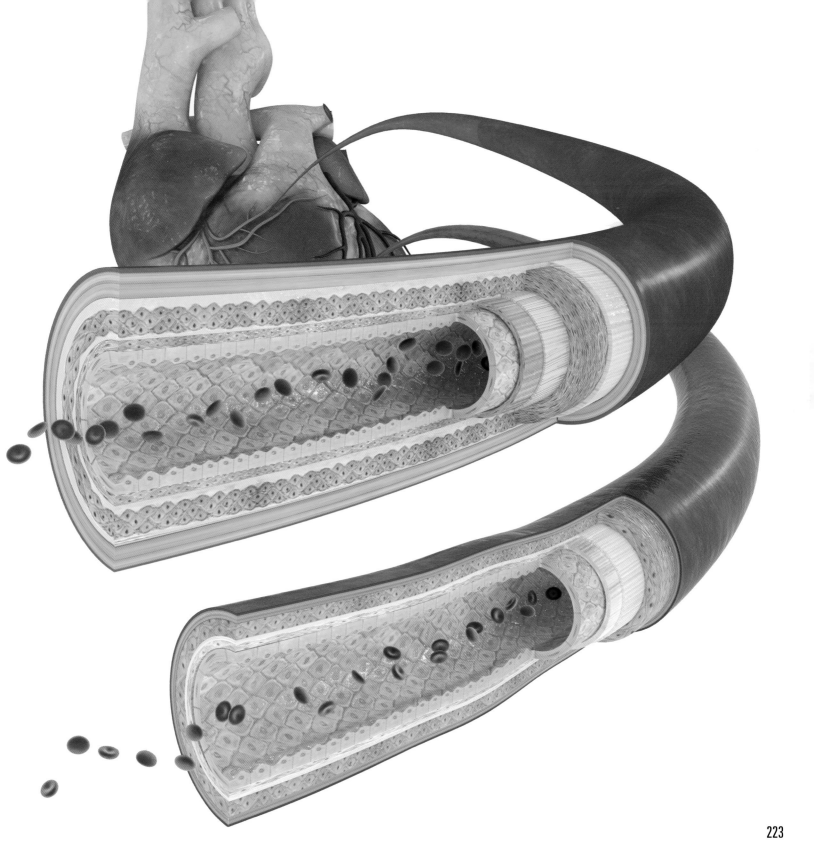

You can go **without eating** *for weeks,* but **eleven days** is tops for going *without sleep.*

ONCE YOU START
HICCUPPING,
YOU WILL USUALLY
HICCUP AT LEAST
63 TIMES
BEFORE YOU STOP.

The liver is the SECOND LARGEST ORGAN, after the skin.

HUMANS SPEND ⅓ OF THEIR LIVES SLEEPING.

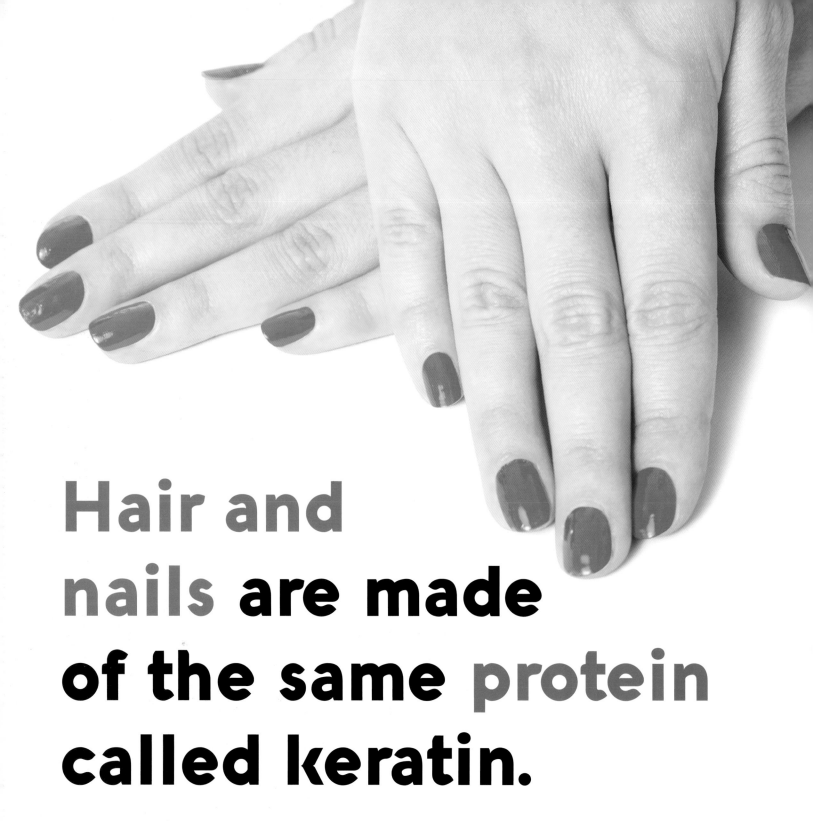

Hair and nails are made of the same protein called keratin.

The egg is the largest single cell in the female human body. It can be seen with the naked eye.

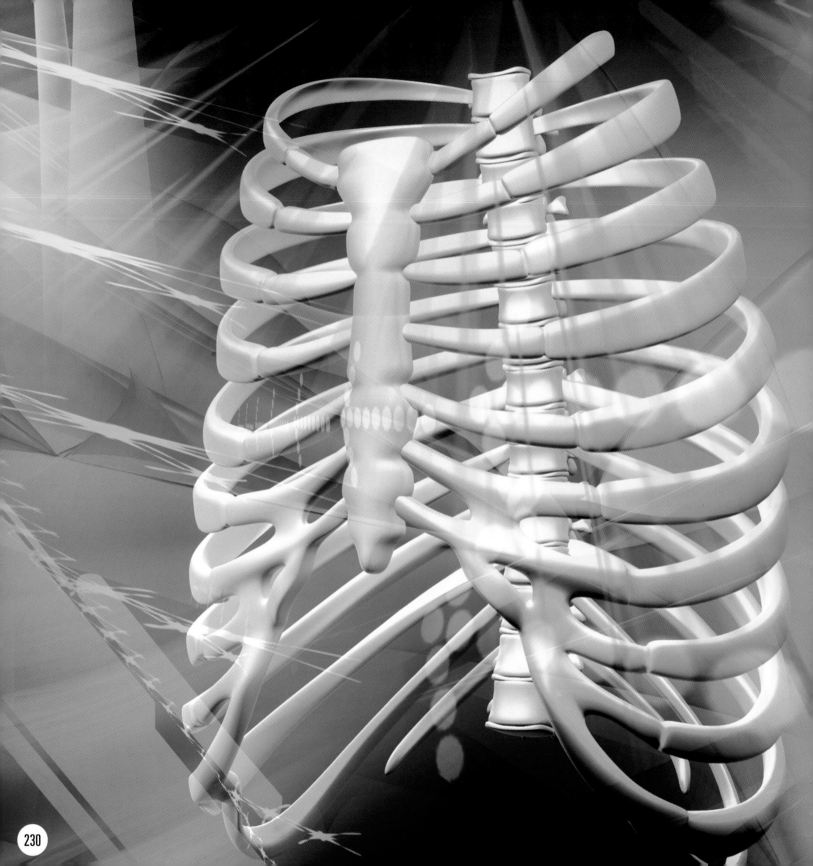

A TYPICAL HUMAN RIBCAGE IS MADE UP OF 24 RIBS.

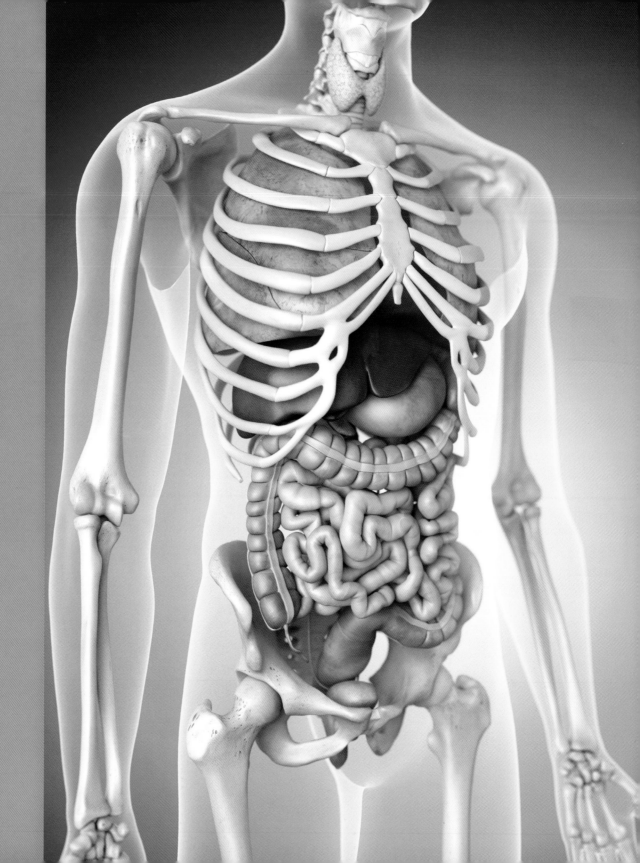

One person in every 10,000 is born with his/her major organs mirrored/flipped.

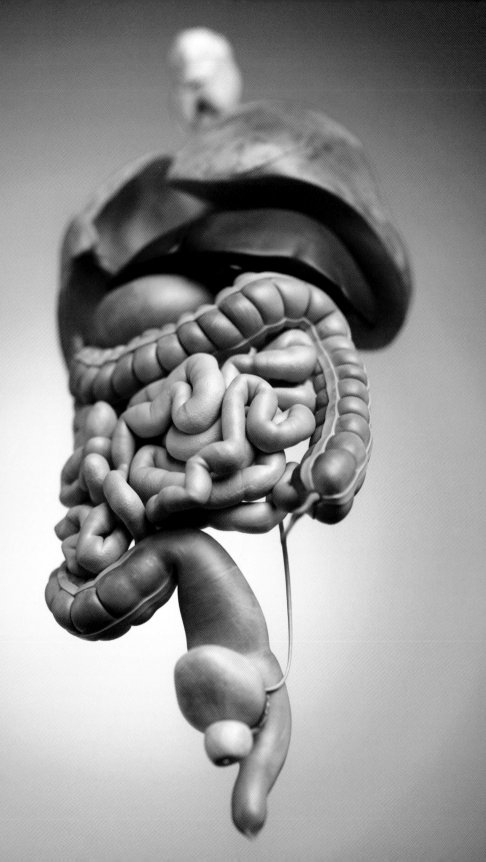

This is called situs inversus.

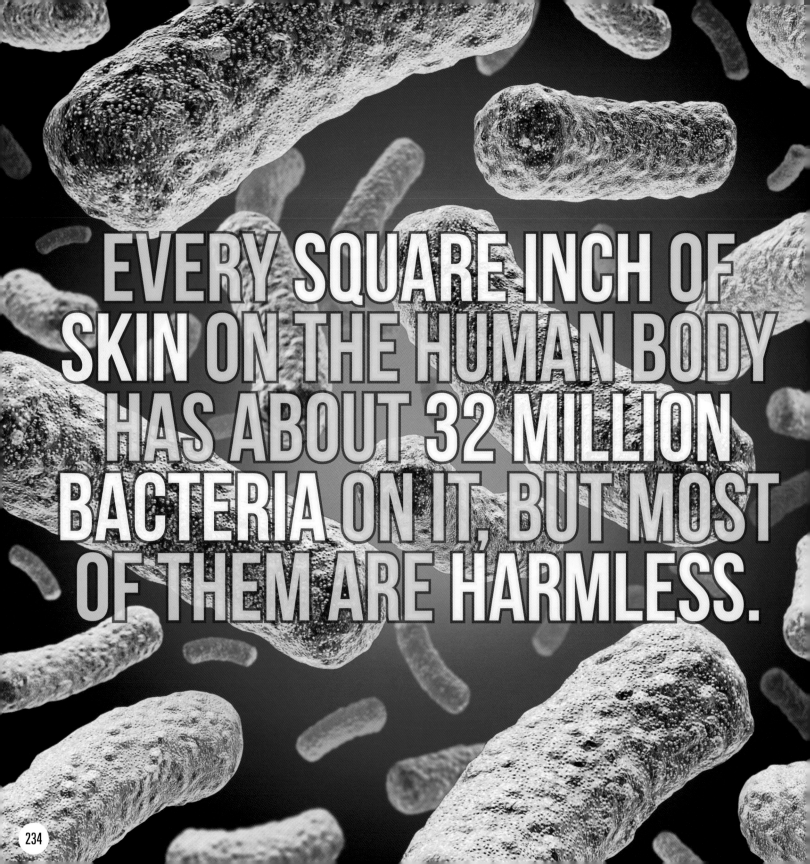

EVERY SQUARE INCH OF SKIN ON THE HUMAN BODY HAS ABOUT 32 MILLION BACTERIA ON IT, BUT MOST OF THEM ARE HARMLESS.

THE PANCREAS HELPS CONTROL YOUR BLOOD SUGAR LEVELS.

Women's hearts beat FASTER than men's, but men have LARGER hearts.

The outside of teeth, called enamel, is the hardest part of your body.

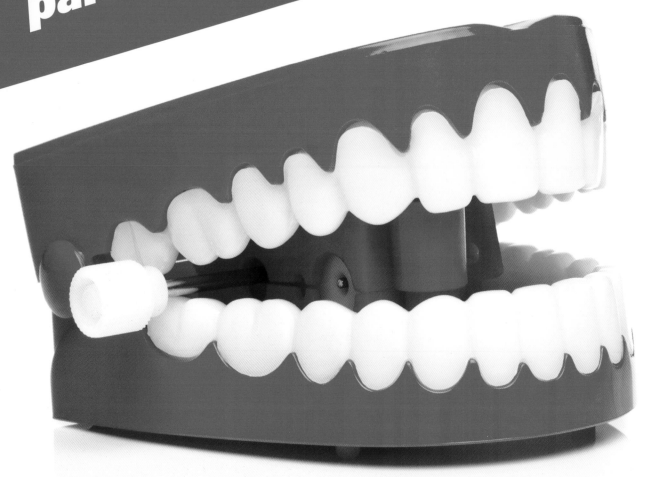

PICA IS THE CONDITION OF CRAVING NON-FOOD ITEMS LIKE HAIR, CHALK, AND DIRT.

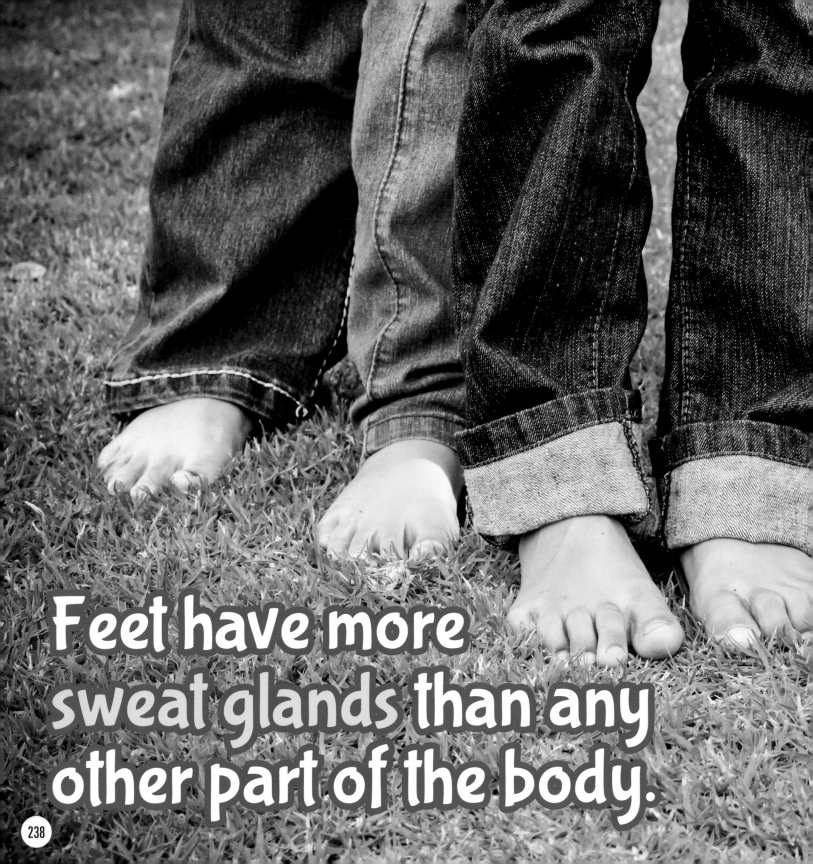

Feet have more sweat glands than any other part of the body.

Right-handed people live an average of nine years longer than left-handed people.

The third finger is known as the ring finger. Women and men will sometimes wear a ring on their left ring finger to show that they are married or engaged.

The technical term for the armpit is **"axilla."**

Sweat is actually **odorless.** It gets its smell from the **bacteria** that live in your skin.

240

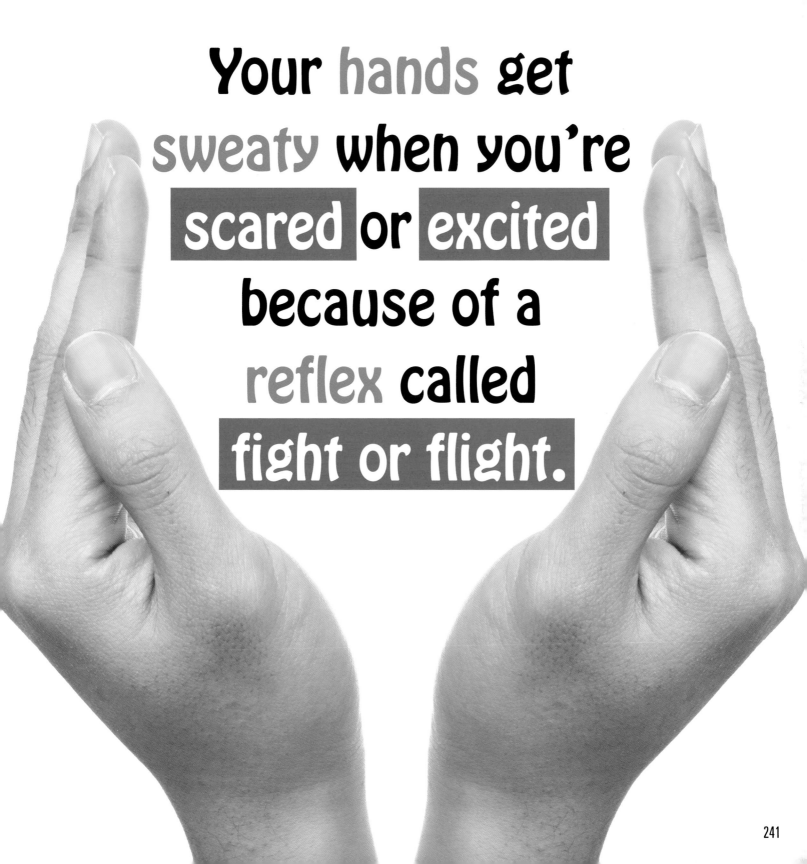

Your hands get sweaty when you're scared or excited because of a reflex called fight or flight.

IT IS IMPOSSIBLE TO SNEEZE WHILE SLEEPING.

THE GAP BETWEEN YOUR NOSE AND UPPER LIP IS CALLED THE PHILTRUM.

The **eye** is made up of **many** different parts, including the **cornea**, iris, lens, and **retina.**

THE CENTRAL NERVOUS SYSTEM IS MADE

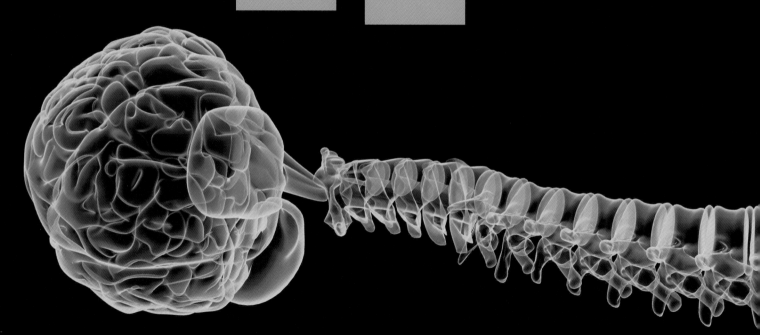

UP OF THE BRAIN AND SPINAL CORD.

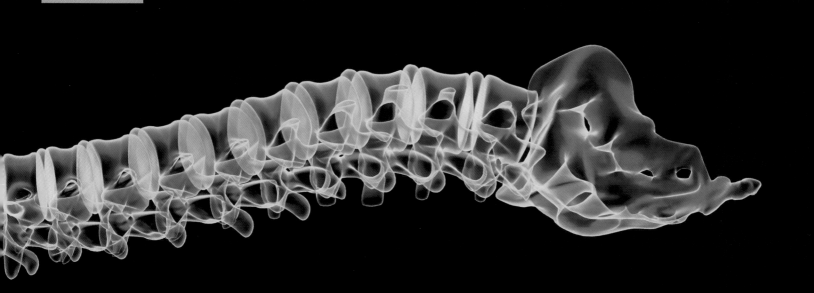

About half the kids in America bite their nails.

MEN USE THE LEFT SIDE OF THEIR BRAINS TO LISTEN. WOMEN USE BOTH SIDES.

Your small intestine is anywhere from 18 to 23 feet long.

THE HUMAN BRAIN IS MADE OF 60% FAT.

It takes longer to lose muscle than to gain it.

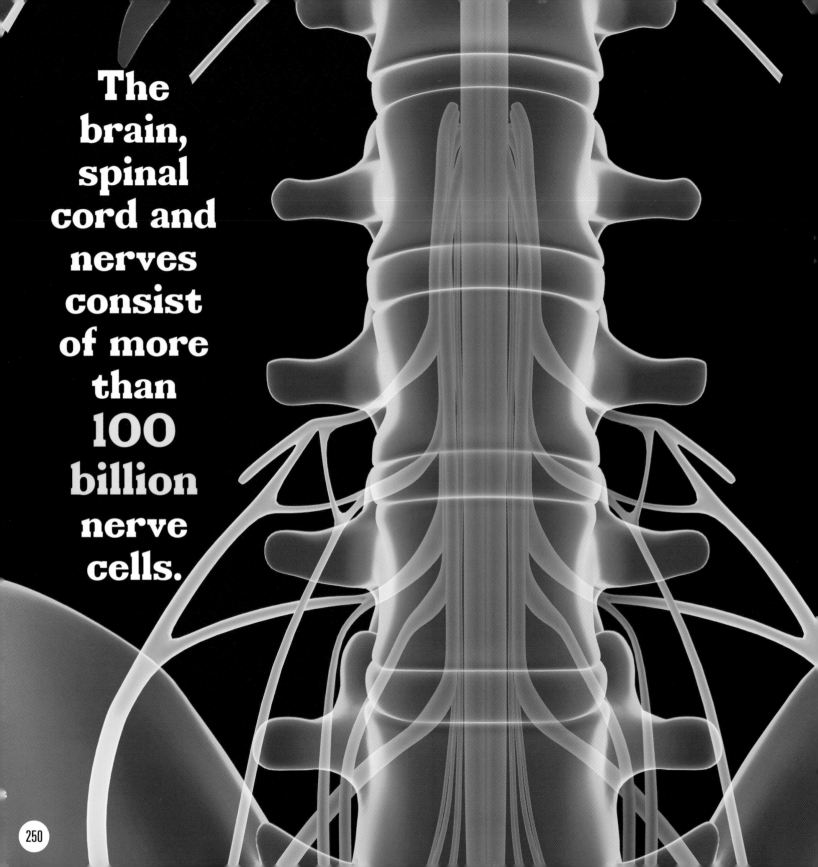

The brain, spinal cord and nerves consist of more than 100 billion nerve cells.

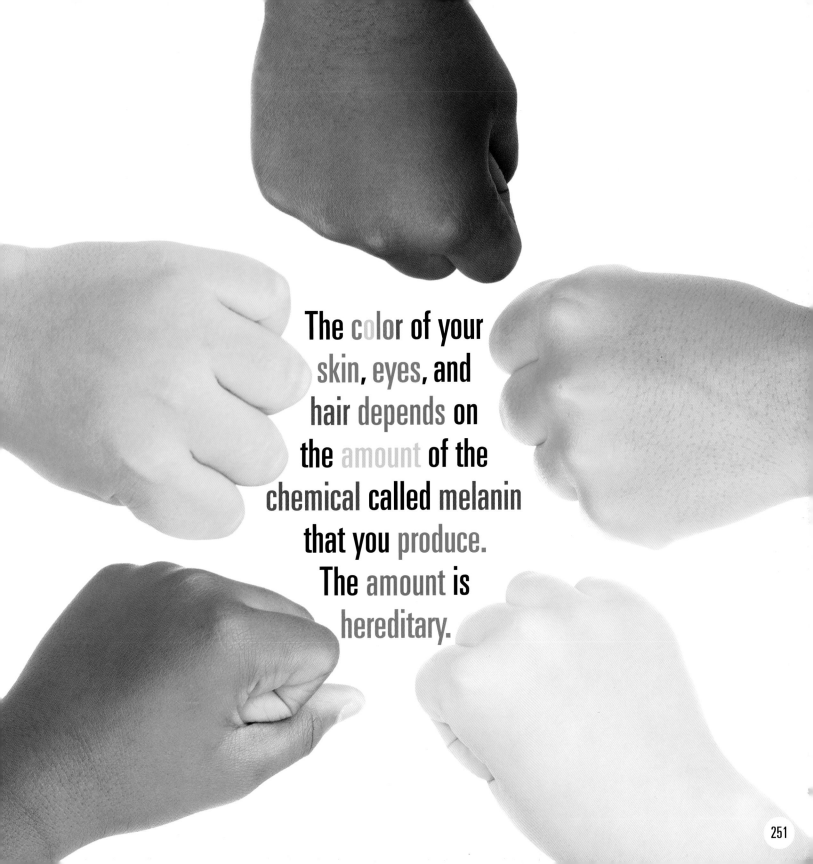

The color of your skin, eyes, and hair depends on the amount of the chemical called melanin that you produce. The amount is hereditary.

There is no scientific word for the skin of the elbow.

THE HUMAN HEART CREATES ENOUGH PRESSURE WHEN IT PUMPS OUT OF THE BODY TO SQUIRT BLOOD 30 FEET.

The body has enough IRON in it to make a NAIL measuring three inches long.

The weight of the adult human brain is three pounds.